FORBIDDEN PSYCHOLOGY

Beyond Mind Games - The Complete Guide to Discover Techniques of Mass Manipulation and Subdue Anyone's Mind through Subliminal Persuasion and Dark NLP

by

Blake Reyes

TABLE OF CONTENTS

INTRODUCTION

The aura that covers the forbidden is irresistible. Seduced people are not satisfied until they fulfill the desires that the unallowed situations awaken. If they fail to achieve them, they fall into the eternal question: "What if I had done it?" Living forever in these illusions.

According to psychology, it is natural that people want to stop curiosity and, mainly, try new things because freedom, security, and independence are the most delicious. Just like the biblical story that says that Eve did not resist temptation and tasted the forbidden fruit, we also always have many forbidden fruits that arouse will. We constantly imagine the pleasure they can provide us.

This happens right from birth where, at each moment, the human being is in constant learning about the moral, ethical, and social limits, each one with its values and rules. Thus, the child is always learning what is right or wrong, and the first people who will dictate this path are parents and, soon after, society, which continues to inject limits and points that cannot be overcome.

Consequently, our condition and prohibition lead us to experiment, and attract us to what is denied; after all, the forbidden is better. This is because we always need to know more and test how far we can go, get to know new airs, to venture out, even if later we will face the consequences.

Want to be more lovable, valued, admired, cherished, and worshiped? Do you feel like people are manipulating you, and making you do things you don't want to do?

Are you sick and tired of having someone taking advantage? Do you want to stand up, be in control, and never feel disrespected?

What if I told you I could make you a master persuader who can almost easily and most importantly... unknowingly get everything you want?

Here's a preview of the important techniques that you'll learn from this book:

Convince even the world's most stubborn guy, and make him almost blindly obey your commands!

Make friends everywhere you go – it's easy to learn some "mind-tricks" that you will enjoy anywhere.

Make anyone follow your orders so quietly that they won't even know what's going on.

"The Secrets of Manipulation" will teach you tested techniques to win every debate!

Methods of Persuasion.

Gain control of ANY social circle Instantly.

How to get the truth out of someone at any time.

How to say thrilling and attentive stories.

How to turn yourself into a super positive person and make others appealing to you!

The technique to convince and PERSUADE effectively.

Be irresistibly attractive and interesting to others.

CHAPTER 1

FORBIDDEN PSYCHOLOGY

Psychology is a study of mental processes and human comportment, according to the American Psychological Association (APA). Therefore, psychology refers to the study of the mind, how it functions, and how it influences human actions.

The study of psychology encompasses all facets of human life, from brain functions to countries' behavior, from child growth to caring for the elderly, and from scientific research centers to mental health programs, "understanding behavior" is the role of psychologists in the most varied contexts. (APA)

Psychologists and psychiatrists work together to support people with mental health problems, but they are not the same. While the psychologist treats a patient through psychotherapy, helping to relieve symptoms through behavioral changes, the psychiatrist, who is a doctor specializing in psychiatry, focuses more on prescribing medications and other interventions to manage mental health conditions.

Psychology is now considered to be the science that studies the human "mind" and behavior. Being both an area of activity (applied science) and a field of research (academic science), psychology studies human behavior and the functioning of the human mind, that is, how conscious, and unconscious cognitive processes influence how we make decisions and behave.

As a multifaceted discipline, psychology includes many sub-fields of study such as human development, sport, mental health, clinical, social, community behavior, and cognitive processes, to name a few.

The researchers of psychology aim to understand and explain how thoughts, behaviors, and emotions work.

Now, what is forbidden psychology?

Forbidden psychology is a term for explaining Psychology's dark side. It revolves around all of the things culture is warning us not to do. Those are things the UN and Genova organisations regulate and prohibit.

If someone has the mandate to understand how and why we humans are doing what we are doing, they may use it against others. Here are some of the other things you can do if you are aware of forbidden psychology:

- Manipulation
- Mind control
- Emotional Seduction
- Mental abuse
- Deception
- Brainwashing
- Torture

Now all of the above things look negative and cruel to someone. The truth is that life is harsh too, and someone can know about this stuff, and then use it against you.

Learning about forbidden psychology is important because people use it to trick the mind. That's a good way to think about studying or reading this. You may get a sense of when someone wants to exploit you or abuses you emotionally or uses brainwashing to seduce you. People also use the methods to prosecute and torment people across the globe.

History Of Dark Psychology And How It Applies In Real Life

Dark Psychology is Human Condition Research. It applies to people's psychological nature of preying on other people driven by criminal and deviant drives that lack intent, general theories of instinctual drives and the theory of social science. All humanity can hurt other human beings and living creatures. Although this urge is restrained or sublimated by others, some act upon such impulses.

Dark Psychology attempts to explain certain emotions, feelings, beliefs, and mechanisms of subjective thinking that contribute to aggressive actions and are antithetical to contemporary human behavioral understandings. Dark Psychology believes that violent, deviant, and abusive activities are purposive, and 99.99 percent have some logical, goal-oriented motivation. It is the remaining sections of .01 percent that make up Dark Psychology from Adlerian theory and Teleology. There is an area within the human psyche that Dark Psychology postulates, causing certain individuals to perform atrocious actions without intent. In this hypothesis, the Dark Singularity was coined.

Dark Psychology posits that all humankind has a reservoir of malevolent intent toward others ranging from minimally obtrusive and fleeting thoughts to utter psychopathic deviant behavior without any clear cause. This is called the Dark Spectrum. It is mitigating influences that serve as accelerators and attractants to reach the Dark Singularity. The heinous acts of an individual that fall into the Dark Spectrum is what Dark Psychology calls Dark Cause. Below is a brief introduction to certain definitions.

Dark Psychology is not only our moon's dark side but the combination of all moons' dark side.

Dark Psychology includes all that makes us who we are, linked to our dark side. This proverbial cancer is present in all cultures, all religions, and all of humanity. From the moment we come into being, until the time of death, inside us, there is a side lurking that some have called evil, and others have described as criminal, deviant and pathological. Dark Psychology presents a third philosophical construct that takes a different view of these behaviors from religious dogmas and theories of contemporary social science.

It is the one who is not interested in his fellow men who has the greatest difficulties in life and who gives others the greatest injury. It is from these men that all human weaknesses spring up.

Some people commit these same actions in dark psychology positing and doing so for power, money, sex, revenge, or other known purposes. Without a target, they commit those horrid acts. Simplified, the end doesn't justify the means. There are people who, for the sake of doing so, abuse and harm others. The capacity lies inside all of us. The field examined here is the potential to damage others without intent, reason, or intention. Dark Psychology believes that this dark potentiality is extremely elusive and much harder to describe.

Dark Psychology believes that we all have the capacity for predator behaviors, and the capacity has access to our emotions, feelings, and beliefs. We all have this ability as you can read in this text, but only a handful of us act upon them. At one time or another, we all had thoughts and emotions about having to act harshly. We have always had thoughts that we want to harm others without mercy seriously. If you're frank with yourself, you'll have to admit that you've had thoughts and felt like you want to commit evil deeds.

Because of the truth, we consider ourselves to be a kind of benign species; one would like to think that such thoughts and feelings do not exist. Unfortunately, all of us have these ideas, and fortunately, never act upon them. Dark Psychology suggests that there are people who have the same ideas, emotions, and experiences but act upon them deliberately or impulsively. The apparent difference is that they act upon them when others have merely vague thoughts and emotions.

Dark Psychology claims that this type of predator is purposive and has some logical, purpose-oriented motivation. Religion, philosophy, psychology, and other dogmas have been convincing in their attempts to describe

Dark Psychology. It is true that most human behavior, linked to evil acts, is purposeful and purpose-oriented, but Dark Psychology suggests an environment where purposeful behavior and purpose-oriented motivation tend to become nebulous. There is a continuum of victimization of dark psychology, ranging from thoughts to pure psychopathic deviance, with no apparent rationality or purpose. This spectrum, Dark Spectrum, allows the Dark Psychology theory to be conceptualized.

Dark Psychology discusses the aspect of the human psyche or universal human condition that enables sexual behavior and can even animate it. Many of the behavioral patterns' features are its lack of apparent moral purpose, its universality, and its lack of predictability in certain cases. This basic human condition is believed by Dark Psychology to be special or an extension of evolution. Let's look at some very simple evolutionary tenets. Next, remember that we evolved from other animals and are the perfection of all animal life. Our frontal lobe allowed us to become the creature at the apex. Now let us presume that being alpha predators doesn't exempt us from our animal instincts and predatory behavior.

When animals hunt, the smallest, weakest, or females in the group are always stalked and killed. While this fact sounds psychopathic, it is because of their chosen victims that their own risk of injury or death is subdued. All animal life act and behave in that way. All of their barbaric, aggressive, and bloody acts contribute to evolutionary theory, natural selection, and survival and reproductive instinct. There are no aspects of Dark Psychology for the rest of life on our planet. We, human beings, are the ones who embody what Dark Psychology is seeking to discover.

When we look at the human experience, theories of evolution, natural selection, and animal behavior, their abstract tenets appear to disappear. We are the only beings on the planet's face to prey on one another for the species' survival without the excuse of procreation. Human beings are the only species that prey unexplained desires upon others. Dark Psychology discusses the aspect of the human psyche or universal human condition that enables sexual behavior and can even compel it. Dark Psychology believes that there is something intrapsychic that drives and is anti-evolutionary to our behavior. Humans are the only species to murder each other for reasons other than life, food, land, or procreation.

Dark Psychology also believes that this dark side is unpredictable. Unpredictable in understanding who is acting on these dangerous impulses, and even more unpredictable in the lengths some will go completely negated with their sense of mercy. Some people rape, assassinate, torture, and violate without cause or intent. Dark Psychology speaks of behaving like a predator, pursuing human prey without clearly specified reasons for such acts. We are extremely dangerous to ourselves as human beings and to any other living being. The reasons for this are numerous and Dark Psychology attempts to investigate certain dangerous elements.

Important Concepts Of Dark Psychology

The more readers can understand Dark Psychology, the

more prepared they are to their chances of being victimized by human predators. It is necessary to have at least a minimum understanding of Dark Psychology before proceeding. Six tenets are required to understand Dark Psychology thoroughly, as follows:

1. Dark Psychology is a part of the human experience as a whole. This build has exerted historical influence. All cultures, communities, and the people who live in them maintain this aspect of human nature. According to the most compassionate men, they have this evil domain, but never act upon it and have lower levels of violent feelings and thoughts.

2. Dark Psychology is Human Condition Research, as it relates to the emotions, feelings, and beliefs of people linked to this inherent capacity to prey on others without simple definable motives. As all action is purposeful, goal-oriented, and conceptualized by modus operandi, Dark Psychology puts forth the notion that the closer a person comes to the "black hole" of pure evil, the less likely he/she has a motivational purpose. While some believe that pure evil is never achieved, Dark Psychology claims that some are coming close since it is infinite.

3. In its latent form, Dark Psychology may be underestimated due to its potential for misinterpretation as aberrant psychopathy. History is full of examples of this latent propensity to manifest itself as aggressive, destructive behavior. Current psychiatry and psychology describe the psychopath as an unrepentant abuser for his actions. There is a spectrum of intensity Dark Psychology

posits, ranging from thoughts and feelings of violence to extreme victimization and abuse without rational intent or motivation.

4. In this spectrum, Dark Psychology's intensity is not judged less or more horrific by victimization behavior but maps out a variety of inhumanity. Comparing Ted Bundy and Jeffrey Dahmer will be an easy example. Both psychopaths were serious, and their acts were heinous. The difference is that Dahmer committed his atrocious assassinations for his misguided desire for companionship while Ted Bundy was assassinated and sadistically caused suffering from pure psychopathic cruelty. On the Dark Spectrum, both will be higher, but Jeffrey Dahmer can be best understood by his desperate psychotic desire to be accepted.

5. Dark Psychology believes that every human being has a capacity for aggression. This ability is innate in all humans, and multiple internal and external influences increase the risk of development of this ability through unpredictable behaviors. Such actions are fundamentally aggressive, and may often act without purpose. Dark Psychology claims individual interpretations of the predator-prey relationship. Dark Psychology is simply a human phenomenon and no other living being experiences it. In other living organisms, aggression and mayhem occur, but humans are the only species that can do so without intent.

6. An awareness of Dark Psychology's underlying causes and triggers would help enable society to identify, treat, and potentially minimize the dangers inherent in its impact.

Learning Dark Psychology concepts serves a twofold purpose, which is beneficial. First, recognizing that we all have the capacity for bad, those with this information will reduce the risk of it erupting. Second, understanding Dark Psychology's tenets ties in with our original evolutionary intent of striving to survive.

CHAPTER 2

FUNDAMENTALS IN PERSUASION

In this chapter, we introduce the notion of persuasion, whose field of study, history, and the scope of the disciplines and concepts involved are much larger than this chapter's subject, namely technological persuasion. On the other hand, it is the essential starting point for any study on the subject. First to understand the role played by technology, that of the persuader (i.e., what should be its characteristics?). Then to understand the action that exercises this technology on the user, namely the persuasion process (i.e., what are the persuasion techniques?). Finally to understand the impact of this action on the user and the mechanisms at work in the latter, the persuaded (i.e., understanding these mechanisms to optimize the action of persuasive technology).

First, we briefly recall the history of the concept of persuasion over the centuries, then we define the main terms related to this activity. Finally, we recall the main theories developed in the context of psychology to account for human activity.

Historical roots

Persuasion has a long history in the West, which is rooted in Greek and Roman antiquity. Under the name of rhetoric, it was an integral part of the education of the children of the elite of the Greek cities. Knowing how to influence crowds, inspire emotions, change opinions, or motivate to act, was an art deployed during speeches within the agora or the forum. The mastery of eloquence was even seen as the key to maintaining a healthy democracy.

In antiquity, persuasion was closely linked to philosophy. If the debate, dear to Plato, aims at establishing knowledge through dialogue or the examination of distinct positions, rhetoric focuses less on the discovery of truth than on the ability to influence by the speech. Aristotle, the disciple of Plato and tutor of Alexander the Great, devotes three books to rhetoric. He then defines it as "the faculty of considering, for each question, what can be persuasive." Later, Schopenhauer will say in the art of being always right, that "we can indeed be objectively right about the debate itself while being wrong in the eyes of those present, and sometimes even in our own eyes."

In ancient Rome, Cicero was the main theorist of rhetoric and argumentation. He devotes many treatises to the art of oratory based in particular on his experience as a lawyer and politician. For Cicero, a speech must fulfill three functions: to instruct, please, and move.

These works of ancient philosophers will be a reference for many centuries to come. It was not until the 17th century, notably with Francis Bacon, René Des-Cartes, or John Locke, to distance itself from Aristotelian concepts. If this is not strictly speaking rhetoric, Descartes' rationalism and the empiricism of Bacon and Locke will profoundly change the way of understanding knowledge and of arguing. By defining reason and experience respectively as the source of knowledge, they will allow the sciences to develop outside the fields of theology and metaphysics and open the way to modern sciences.

It is one of those sciences, psychology, which from the beginning of the 20th century, will produce most of our knowledge on behavior, attitude, and how to influence them. As in antiquity, interest in persuasion is not uncorrelated from public life. For example, ambitious research programs have been implemented in social psychology to determine the causes of changes in attitude and behavior to meet the American government's need to convince its citizens to support the war effort. Hovland and the Yale school thus discovered several decisive results in persuasions, such as the importance of the source's credibility, the content of the argument, or the channel conveying the persuasive message. The results obtained in psychology also find concrete applications in marketing, advertising, or even education, areas where the ability to influence can be decisive. These disciplines have managed to appropriate this knowledge and go beyond it by developing theories and models dedicated to their fields of action.

Definitions

In this section, we study the definitions of persuasion, and the two main concepts it manipulates are behavior and attitude.

Persuasion

The first difficulty in defining persuasion is identifying its purpose. If the most common acceptance sees persuasion as a means of influencing others, its actions, beliefs, and desires, some limit its field of action to attitudes. The change in behavior is then seen only as a consequence of the change of perspective about the object of attitude, just as can be the emotions. Thus, Petty and Cacioppo define persuasion as "a change in beliefs and attitudes resulting from exposure to communication."

If there is a difference of finality in the definitions of persuasion, there is also a difference in the processes implemented to achieve this finality. In its broadest sense, all means are good for managing to influence others. Romma thus indicates that it can be "linguistic, argumentative or psychological processes such as seduction or manipulation, up to body language, images, etc." She adds that persuasion can "be direct and explicit or, conversely, implicit conveying meaning in a disguised manner." On the other hand, in a more restricted view, the change of attitude or behavior must be voluntary and conscious. In this view, persuasion can be compared to communication. An author communicates a message, via a channel, to a target that processes this message to possibly modify his beliefs or actions. Each element in this chain of communication is important to the success of persuasion. Lasswell sums it up by the question "Who says what, by which channel, to whom, in what channel and with what effect?", called in English the 5W (Who says What to Whom in What channel with What effect?). Perlo thus defines persuasion as "a symbolic process in which communicators try to convince people to change their attitudes or behaviors about a subject by transmitting a message in an atmosphere of free choice." Petty and Cacioppo's definition also corresponds to this restricted vision of persuasion, even if it limits finality to attitudes.

By adopting this strict perspective, persuasion is not the only way to change attitude and behavior. For Girandola, the two main methods studied in psychology to influence others' attitudes or behavior are persuasion and commitment. If persuasion, in the strict sense, influences behavior through attitude, engagement does the opposite. It is based on the need for coherence in individuals between thought and action by encouraging them to make their attitudes conform to specific behaviors. Kiesler defines engagement as "a bond that unites the individual to his behavioral acts." We will detail a little more in the chapter engagement dedicated to the theory of cognitive dissonance to which it is attached. Note that persuasion in the broad sense includes engagement.

Other methods of influencing behavior exist. Through an analysis of nineteen frameworks dedicated to behavior change, Michie et al., for example, identified nine behavioral influence methods, which they grouped under the term behavior change wheel. Beyond persuasion and commitment, this behavior change wheel identifies:

- Education: "increasing knowledge and understanding."
- The incentive: "to create an expectation of reward."
- Coercion: "create an expectation of punishment or

cost."

- Training: "transmitting skills."
- The restriction: "using rules to reduce the opportunities to practice the behavior."
- Restructuring of the environment: "to modify the physical or social context."
- Modeling: "provide an example that inspires, that people imitate."
- Facilitation: "increase resources and reduce barriers to the practice of behavior."

Many of these techniques can be thought of like persuasion, in its broadest definition. For example, Fogg, a precursor of technological persuasion, integrates them all into this discipline except coercion, because for him, even if coercion can lead to a change in behavior through the use of force (or at least threat), it cannot be assimilated to persuasion which implies a framework of freedom. He thus defines persuasion as "an attempt to change attitudes, behavior, or both simultaneously, without the use of coercion or deception."

Behavior

The definition of the concept of behavior seems to elicit little debate in the literature. The great dictionary of psychology defines it, for example, as "the set of objectively observable reactions that an organism, generally provided with a nervous system, executes in response to the environment's stimuli, themselves objectively observable."

Attitude

As early as 1935, Allport made an attitude "the most distinctive and indispensable concept of contemporary social psychology." At the beginning of the 20th century, it is first apprehended as "emotion or a thought comprising a motor (or behavioral) component." The link between attitude and behavior is therefore identified very early on as fundamental. Subsequently, two other dimensions complete the definition of attitude: the cognitive component which makes the attitude a knowledge or a belief towards an object of attitude (i.e., a person, a physical object, a concept, a behavior, ...), and the affective component which makes the attitude an evaluation, positive or negative of the object of attitude. For Rosenberg and Hovland, "attitudes can be conceptualized as cognitive, affective, and behavioral components consistent with one another. For a given object, beliefs and knowledge about the object, the evaluation of this object, and the behaviors resulting from it are consistent in the same individual.

Others prefer to retain only the attitude component, the cognitive and behavioral components being the only secondary in their eyes. The attitude is then above all an evaluation towards an object, a concept, an action, or an individual. These different points of view are explained by the fact that an attitude is not directly observable. It is by his way of acting, expressing himself, or expressing an emotion that we can assess an individual's attitude.

However, in its effective component, the link between behavior and attitude is not always as obvious as the definition of Rosenberg and Hov-land might suggest, as

Wicker showed. Several explanations for this divergence are then considered: a difficulty in measuring behaviors and attitudes in the experiments studied, the influence of external factors in the choice of behaviors, the competition of several attitudes, or again the need to introduce a notion of strength of attitudes. Fishbein and Ajzen thus propose introducing new factors such as social norms or the perception of control, in competition with attitude to determine behavior. We will study their theory of planned activities in a dedicated chapter.

Another track studied is that of the strength of an attitude. The stronger an attitude, the more resistant it is to change, the more stable it is over time, and the more it influences behavior and cognition. If the cognitive, affective, and behavioral dimensions make it possible to assess the direction of attitude (positive or negative), Krosnick et al. propose ten dimensions to assess their strength:

- Accessibility: "the ease with which an evaluation comes to mind when encountering an object of attitude."
- The extremity: the more important the evaluation of the attitude (towards the negative or towards the positive), the more extreme it is.
- Intensity: identical at the end but for the emotional reaction elicited.
- Certainty: "the degree of confidence given to an attitude."
- Importance: "the subjective perception of interest in an attitude."

- Interest: "the extent to which an object of attitude is hedonically relevant for the holder of the attitude."
- Direct experience: "the more frequently a behavior is expressed, the more accessible the attitude is specific to it."
- Knowledge: the sum of knowledge which supports the attitude
- A structural consistency: "a close relationship between the feeling towards the object and the beliefs about its attributes."
- The latitude of rejection and non-engagement: "the more an individual opposes or rejects the arguments put forward in a message, the clearer his initial attitude."

Theories and models of behavior

In this section, we wish to study human behavior, particularly how each individual determines his actions and is likely to be influenced by a persuasive attempt. For this purpose, psychology is an unavoidable discipline. For more than a century now, human beings in general have been studied, and their mental processes, notably those at work in the development of human behavior. Many models and multiple theories have been proposed, which allow us to anticipate better and grasp human action and its constraints. Even if we cannot be exhaustive, these models and these theories that we wish to explain here, focus on those cited in the section on technological persuasion. We describe the processes it exhibits for each of them, and we illustrate it with a common example: selective sorting of waste.

Operational conditioning

Principle

Conditioning is a learning theory, developed at the beginning of the 20th century by Pavlov. It is built around the link between an environmental stimulus and the reaction it causes in a living being (in a dog in the case of Pavlov's work). This theory is particularly interested in stimuli, classifying them into three categories:

- Neutral stimulus: does not cause behavior.
- Unconditional stimulus: systematically provokes the behavior without prior learning.
- Conditional stimulus: initially neutral, this stimulus causes behavior after the learning phase.

Learning takes place by combining a neutral stimulus with an unconditional stimulus, then suppressing the unconditional stimulus to make the neutral stimulus a conditional stimulus. Pavlov thus associated different sounds (neutral stimulus) with the action of feeding his dogs (unconditional stimulus) and measured their salivation (behavior). Once conditioned, the sound alone (conditional stimulus) created salivation (behavior) without bringing food.

Skinner then introduces the notion of operant conditioning, which differs from Pavlovian conditioning by taking into consideration the consequences of behavior. The probability of reproducing the behavior is greater if the consequences of it are perceived as positive by the individual: he anticipates the consequences of the behavior before deciding to adopt it. There are four types of operant conditioning:

- Positive reinforcement: Increases the probability of appearance of behavior following the addition of an appetitive stimulus.
- Negative reinforcement: Increases the probability of the appearance of behavior following the withdrawal of an aversive stimulus.
- Positive punishment: Decreases the probability of a behavior appearing by adding an aversive stimulus.
- Negative punishment: Decreases the probability of the appearance of behavior by the withdrawal of an appetitive stimulus.

As a result of operative conditioning, individuals, subject to a new situation, would learn by series of "trial and error" to establish a map of the consequences and better choose the behavior appropriate to the situation (i.e., the stimulus).

Illustration on selective sorting

An individual can decide whether or not to sort his waste by anticipating the consequences of this behavior. The ecological consequences will favor the sorting of waste, while the anticipation of the additional efforts required by this behavior can curb it.

It is possible to influence the individual by adding positive or negative consequences to the behavior. For example, some municipalities have implemented a tax linked to the weight of unsorted waste (negative reinforcement associated with non-sporting behavior). This incentive could be seen as a positive reinforcement associated with sorting behavior if it took the form of a bonus linked to the sorted waste weight.

Social cognitive theory

Principles

Cognitive, social theory is, in part, a reaction to the behaviorist current of which operant conditioning is a part. It first offers an alternative to learning by trial and error, judging it uneconomical, long and dangerous. Indeed, trying different behaviors in a new situation requires effort, time, and risks in the absence of knowledge about these tested behaviors' consequences.

For Bandura, the preferred learning method for individuals would be observed, which he calls vicarious learning or modeling. However, this observation does not lead to mere mimicry. It is an active observation where the observer filters, interprets, and symbolizes the information he perceives. He assimilates behavior patterns and skills and modifies his motivation to adopt the behavior by interpreting its consequences in the model individual. The characteristics of the model, such as its similarity or its effective proximity to the observer, favor vicarious learning.

Bandura also redefines the place of human beings in action in their environment. The individual is not an automaton reacting to environmental stimuli, as behaviorist theories might lead us to believe. He is an actor in his own life, able to direct the course of his actions. This is what he calls the human agency.

Environmental stimuli undergo the effect of the cognitive processes. They are filtered, analyzed, interpreted before they can have any effect on behavior. The individual anticipates the results of his actions, sets goals, and evaluates his activity in self-regulation of his activity and motivation. Self-regulatory processes act in anticipation and feedback on behavior. The individual develops an objective according to the result he wishes to obtain (anticipated consequences) and his confidence in his capacity to obtain this result (called self-efficiency by Bandura). He self-assesses throughout the activity, comparing his performance to the target. If the goal is achieved, the self-assessment will provide satisfaction to the individual.

Conversely, if the objective is not reached, the individual will feel dissatisfaction. The more ambitious the objective, the greater the satisfaction obtained by achieving the objective. The development of an objective is a source of motivation by the anticipation of the result of the behavior and the anticipation of the satisfaction provided by the self-evaluation. Self-assessment can also provide motivation. In the event of failure to achieve the goal, if the individual maintains their goal, then they will wish to continue or even strengthen their efforts (a manifestation of motivation) to achieve the goal. Maintaining the goal will greatly depend on the individual's confidence in their abilities (self-efficacy). But failure can also lead the individual to discouragement, which will manifest itself in a downward revision of his goal, or even complete abandonment.

Bandura argues that the interactions between behavior, environment, and personal factors form a reciprocal triadic causality. Each of these three elements influences the other two with an intensity that varies according to the situation and according to the activity in progress.

As we have just seen, personal factors influence behavior, in particular, through self-regulatory processes. In return, the behavior can influence personal factors such as effects or cognitions, for example, if the behavior fails.

Interactions between the environment and personal factors can, in one sense, take the form of persuasion or vicarious learning and, in the other, the influence of the individual on his environment outside of his action. Physical characteristics (age, height, gender...) for example, can create reactions and, therefore, modifications in the social environment.

Finally, through his behavior, an individual can affect his environment (for example, moving an object, interacting with someone). In return, the environment can act on behavior (sometimes indirectly, because cognitions mediate it), show the behaviorist theories.

Illustration on selective sorting

If an individual can see another person apply selective sorting to their waste, can observe how he implements it (for example, the use of containers dedicated to recyclable waste, the installation of a composter in the garden,...), and can perceive the benefits that he derives from this behavior (for example, the satisfaction of being more ecological, the reduction of tax on household waste,...), he will be encouraged to adopt the same behavior.

An individual will set the goal of sorting his waste in anticipation of this behavior (for example, more ecological, fewer taxes...). And because he feels capable of sorting (for example, he knows recyclable waste, he knows how to send his waste for recycling...). Subsequently, he self-evaluates his action about the goal he has set for himself. If he considers that he has achieved his goal, he derives satisfaction from it and strengthens his esteem to sort his waste. If he considers that he has not reached his objective, he may abandon it, revise it or, on the contrary, redouble his efforts to achieve it, according to his level of confidence in his capacity to achieve this objective.

Theories of a link between attitude and behavior

Principles

To better understand the link between attitude and behavior, Fishbein and Ajzen propose the theory of reasoned action. This model integrates an intermediate cognition between attitude and behavior, intention, which they identify with motivational factors in favor of behavior. For Ajzen, intention denotes the effort that the individual is willing to put into adopting the behavior.

We find an attitude as one of the two determinants of intention, the second being the social norm. Fishbein and Ajzen define attitude as a personal positive or negative feeling against behavior. This attitude is itself formed from beliefs about the consequences of carrying out the behavior, balanced by the importance of the individual attaching to each of these consequences. The other determinant of intention to act, the social norm, reflects the opinion of the individual's social environment on the adoption of the behavior by the latter. The importance also balances that the individual attaches to it. We then speak of subjective standards.

This model has shown a good ability to predict human behavior in many areas (marketing, management, social psychology, health...). However, it ignores certain antecedents of behavior, those who escape the individual's control, such as the resources, skills, or opportunities necessary for certain behaviors.

To answer this problem, Ajzen proposes a new model, called the theory of planned behavior. She takes up the theory of reasoned action, which she enriches with a new antecedent for intention: the perception of control over behavior.

Perceived control represents the degree of ease or difficulty associated with adopting the behavior. It depends both on the resources available to the individual, his skills, and the environment's opportunities. These are the internal and external constraints to the individual, or more precisely, the individual's perception and importance given to these constraints.

Illustration on selective sorting

It is possible to persuade a person to sort their waste (i.e., get them to intend to sort their waste):

- by making them perceive the advantages of sorting their waste (i.e., changing their attitude towards sorting behavior)
- by encouraging his social environment to put pressure on him to sort his waste
- by making it easier for them to sort their waste by providing suitable containers, for example, or by reassuring them about their ability to adopt this behavior.

Cognitive dissonance

Principles

The theory of reasoned action presents a rational vision of the individual. He would act according to his attitudes. With the theory of cognitive dissonance, Festinger shows that the human being is also a rationalizing being, granting his opinions and beliefs to his actions after the fact. This theory postulates that the dissonance between two cognitions of the individual — in the case that interests us here, his behavior and attitude towards this behavior — creates an emotional discomfort that prompts the individual to reduce the dissonance by modifying the least resistant cognition.

One of the experiments conducted by Festinger to illustrate his theory consists of having an essay written in favor of an attitude contrary to the beliefs of the individual. The evaluation of the attitude after the experience shows an evolution of beliefs in the direction of the opinion defended in the dissertation. Attitude changes afterward to be in line with behavior.

To change behavior or attitude using cognitive dissonance, three phases are necessary:

-   The awakening of dissonance: when two cognitions of the same individual become contradictory.
-   Emotional discomfort: The awakening of dissonance generates a need for change to return to a state of well-being.
-   The reduction of dissonance: can take the form of a change in attitude, a change in behavior, and the identification of an external justification ("I didn't want, I was forced") or in relativizing the behavior, to the point of forgetting it.

Illustration on selective sorting

Asking an individual who is not in favor of selective sorting to sort their waste for some time for an experiment can lead them to revise their opinion and thus become more favorable to selective sorting.

Skills, Motivations and Opportunities

Principles

According to the Motivation - Opportunity - Ability or MOA model, the adoption of behavior by an individual is directly influenced by the individual's motivation to adopt it, moderated by his capacities and the opportunity offered by the environment.

Unlike the other theories cited here, the MOA theory is derived from marketing. It has been implemented to explain, more specifically, the behavior of consumers in the face of advertisements. However, it has since been used in many fields to explain different behaviors, notably technological persuasion.

McKinnis sees motivation as an extension of the notion of consumer involvement. It is "goal-oriented excitement." Ability represents the skills necessary to adopt the behavior. More than ability, Bandura has shown that it is the confidence that individuals have in their skills that truly influences behavior. Finally, the opportunity represents the circumstances favorable to the execution of the behavior, brought to the user's attention. It depends above all on the execution environment of the behavior.

Illustration on selective sorting

The probability that an individual will sort their waste depends on:

- his motivation: does he want to sort his waste?
- his skill: does he have the skills and knowledge to sort his waste?
- opportunities offered by the environment: does his physical and social environment allow him to sort his waste?

Information processing

Principle

The model of the probability of elaboration and the model of systematic heuristic information processing are two theories, very close to each other, which study the analysis of persuasive messages by individuals and their impact on their attitudes. According to these two models, two modes of information processing would be used:

- The systematic or "main" mode is characterized by an analysis of the message's semantic content. The resulting judgment will, therefore, depend on the quality of the arguments.

- The heuristic or "peripheral" mode is based on rules, patterns that allow the individual to develop an attitude while minimizing the effort of message analysis. It is not the content of the message and its analyzed arguments, but indices peripheral to the message and information related to the transmission context. For a heuristic to be used by the individual, it must be available in memory, and the index that activates it must appear during the transmission of the message. A typical example of heuristics is "if the message is from an expert, then it is true." The source's expertise index could be a title or a particular outfit, for example. Peripheral indices generally relate to:

- The characteristics of the source of the message: identity, credibility, physical appeal, emotional state. . .

- The behaviors and opinions of the social environment about the object of attitude to which the message relates: opinion of an individual, spontaneous reaction of an audience, and a survey.

- The properties, non-semantic characteristics of the message: its length, number of arguments, speech speed,

medium, and typography.

Individuals process information according to the principle of least cognitive effort (for better optimization of cognitive resources) and suspense (i.e., sufficient confidence in the judgment resulting from the processing of information about the goal pursued). The more the individual has the capacities and the motivation to process the message, the more he is willing to provide efforts for this processing. Therefore, the more he favors the systematic mode.

However, heuristic and systematic processing are not exclusive. An individual generally uses two types of processing, favoring one type rather than another depending on his cognitive abilities, motivation to process the message, and the availability in memory of the heuristics and knowledge that apply to the message and the context. It gradually incorporates the results of the various treatments and assesses the opinion it builds on the attitude object (from evaluating each treatment). If the confidence in this opinion is not sufficient, he seeks to enrich it with new heuristic or systematic treatments until he obtains sufficient confidence in his evaluation of the object of attitude. The level of confidence that he considers necessary will depend on his motivation, which characterizes the importance he attaches to the attitude he builds.

Illustration on selective sorting

An individual can change their opinion to favor selective sorting if they believe the arguments presented to them are relevant, but other factors can modify their judgment. For example:

- Is his interlocutor credible?
- Does he feel close, similar to his interlocutor?
- Did the individuals present to adopt the opinion of their interlocutors?
- Is the number of arguments presented important?

Therefore, the history of persuasion spans more than 2000 years, calling on a wide spectrum of disciplines and presenting multiple fields of application. Because of this richness, the definitions of the concept of persuasion are numerous. As part of the study of persuasive technologies, we adopt that proposed by the precursor of this discipline, namely BJ Fogg. Persuasion is then "an attempt to change attitudes, behavior, or both at the same time, without the use of coercion or deception. This definition has the advantage of targeting both attitude and behavior (not limited to attitude), and of including a large number of means to achieve this (all except coercion and deception for ethical reasons), leaving by extension a wide spectrum of fields of application and a wide choice of implementation available to persuasive technologies.

In technological persuasion, this preliminary passage through persuasion, and a fortiori through psychology and its many theories on human behavior, is rich in lessons. This lighting influences our way of apprehending the user and conceiving the interaction between him and the persuasive system. Thus, it seems important to us to avoid two pitfalls. The first is to see the user as submissive to his environment, be it physical, social, and technological. It, therefore, seems illusory to aim for a total efficiency of a persuasive device which does not know how to take into account the particularities of each of these users, and the singularity of the situation in which he finds himself (in the same way as traditional persuasion is not always a successful activity either).

Likewise, the user should not be seen as a rational being, who would only practice the behaviors he wishes to practice, and all the behaviors he wishes to practice. The reasons which explain the non-adoption of a behavior can be numerous (low motivation, little confidence in its capacity to adapt it, the influence of the social environment, insufficient resources and opportunities, ...), and do not show a hostile attitude towards the behavior or an absence of interest in its adoption. It is not a binary situation where the user completely rejects the behavior, in thought as in act, or conversely adopts it. More generally, the study of models and theories relating to human behavior has shown us that the factors influencing behavior are numerous and that persuasive situations are complex. Therefore, it seems important for us to take this complexity into account in the design and implementation of persuasive technology to optimize its efficiency.

CHAPTER 3

THE PSYCHOLOGY OF PERSUASION

In general, persuasion can be understood as a form of strategic communication that aims to convince other people. Through persuasion, it is possible to induce someone to assume a certain position, perform a specific task, or accept an idea.

This communication includes an adequate posture, emotional appeals, and, mainly, a strong and logical argument. In this way, it is easy to see that the psychology of persuasion is associated with basic topics such as knowledge, rhetoric, and image.

This competence is important for everyone, regardless of profession or industry, but it becomes even more essential for leadership positions, sales professionals, and those who work on projects. And, like most behavioral skills, it can be assimilated and improved.

The Psychology Of Persuasion

In the book "The psychology of persuasion," author Robert Cialdini states that the individual can develop this communication capacity to persuade others' actions and decisions.

Based on his studies, Robert Cialdini created the persuasive communication theory, which is based on the concept of taking advantage of some patterns of conduct internalized collectively, to suggest behaviors. This theory lists the six principles of the psychology of persuasion, which can be taught, learned, and applied:

- **Reciprocity:**

The theory determines that people are more likely to respond to an offer when they have already received something in exchange. Social norms encourage us to respond positively to those who have done us a favor or helped us at some other time.

- **Consistency:**

The individual is also more likely to follow a pattern if he thinks that this model is consistent with his ideals and values.

- **Authority:**

According to this principle, the authority and seniority transmitted by the communicator determine factors for others to feel predisposed to approve or validate something. At this point, the communicator's reasoning and stance have special prominence.

- **Social Validation:**

According to Cialdini, the greater the common sense about behavior, the greater the likelihood that someone will adopt attitudes that fit this pattern.

- **Scarcity:**

In this principle, the author reiterates that the charm generated by a product, service, or situation is inversely proportional to its availability. That is, the scarcer, the more relevant.

- **Friendship/friendliness:**

Finally, the sixth principle indicates that people are more inclined to collaborate or agree with others when there is an identification, a friendship relationship, or some attraction.

It is worth remembering that the principles of Robert Cialdini's influence should not be used autonomously, but combined, as part of more efficient and provocative communication.

The Importance Of Empathy

It is worth mentioning that the power of persuasion can only be improved through an additional skill: listening with the sincere intention of understanding the other. Thus, the speech of the broadcaster deserves full attention. It is necessary to understand the message and the lines and everything behind each comment, such as concerns, expectations, and feelings.

Therefore, it is essential to be prepared to listen and, at the same time, collect information, emotions, and impressions.

It is also important to emphasize that knowing how to listen includes rational and emotional aspects, but does not imply agreeing with the other. Differences may remain, but with effective communication, they are better understood.

The Strength Of The Argument

The argument, in turn, is based on coherence and uses real facts to consolidate a thesis. A good argument is full of examples, data, technical studies, research, and comparisons, to prove the truth of a statement or the feasibility of a proposal.

Thus, the communicator can involve others, making everyone start following the same line of reasoning until they are persuaded.

This power of persuasion is significantly increased when the argument is joined with empathy. In this case, it is possible to create a communication that mixes reason and emotion, reaching the main centers of convincing.

Persuasion In The Corporate Universe

It is easy to see that relationships have become increasingly virtual and, often, less productive. This movement is caused not only by the advancement of technology but also by the underutilization of important skills.

Among these skills are empathy and the ability to argue, which can ensure healthier and more collaborative relationships, especially in the corporate environment - where peaceful coexistence between professionals with the most diverse profiles is a basic need.

Individualism has become a major problem, hampering teamwork and collectivity. Therefore, it is necessary to be careful with the virtualization of communication and the almost exclusive use of e-mails, messaging applications, and social networks.

It is also important to consider that dialogue is an efficient way to perceive fears, motivations, and needs, normally hidden in fully digital communication. Personal contact creates ideal conditions for feedback, negotiation, guidance, advice, and convincing.

Also, the correct application of the psychology of persuasion is one of the main characteristics of true leaders, who manage to inspire and engage their teams. Therefore, this issue must be present in the leadership preparation program. With a powerful argument, it is possible to induce critical thinking — a fundamental ingredient for the formation of high-performance teams. The results will be even better if the communicator is recognized for the positive reference that inspires others.

Aspects That Impact The Power Of Persuasion

Some simple aspects can impact the individual's power of persuasion. Therefore, you need to pay attention to the following tips:

- **Posture, gesture, and tone of voice:**

Posture, gestures, and tone of voice are points that generate trust and credibility. Thus, it is necessary to understand these characteristics and adapt to the model imposed by your interlocutor. Eye contact is part of this same tactic, as it ensures greater proximity. With a few attempts, a connection emerges.

- **Language:**

The language must also be adapted to the model of the

interlocutor so that the conversation flows naturally. Also, it is important to reach people's emotions through stimuli aligned with personal desires and goals. These are excellent ways to persuade.

- **Interruptions:**

To be persuasive, it is essential to avoid interruptions. Harsh cuts and conclusions are signs of anxiety and unpreparedness. A productive dialogue demands time, tranquility, and attention.

- **Converging questions:**

The questions help the communicator to keep the conversation focused on their main goal. This attitude contributes to a more dynamic conversation, because, through structured questions, the interlocutor is also invited to rethink his opinions and evaluate new alternatives.

- **Knowledge:**

The sound argument depends on knowledge. Therefore, it is essential to be up to date, have clear answers, understand the events, and interpret data to establish communication strategies.

The principles of the psychology of persuasion are important skills that can be acquired through specific training, discipline, and focus. Adjustments in one's behavior are fundamental in this improvement process, which will reward the achievement of more productive interpersonal relationships — indispensable for a successful career.

CHAPTER 4

WHAT IS SUBLIMINAL PERSUASION?

The term subliminal means under consciousness.

Subliminal manipulation affects people below their conscious consciousness. It affects more people than just words. It's the force behind or beneath the words. It uses the plain word's normal message in combination with a lower level of conscious cognition to influence a person's decision-making or line of thinking effectively.

Why use subliminal persuasion?

The truth is, you can't use it.

You send other messages non-verbally, whether or not you know them, any time you communicate with words. So why not relay both verbally and non-verbally an important sales message?

Yes, subliminal methods of persuasion are your weapons in this modern world. This helps you gain a lead in a competitive market and keeps you ahead of the game. Dave Lakhani, who wrote many books concerning persuasion and power, said:

"It's no longer convincing to persuade that looks like conviction."

If you feel confident about the decision to buy, you buy a chance.

The moral consciousness of your prospects often provides an unconscious dimension of persuasion to start any successful selling interactions.

As salespeople, you give your unconscious mind feelings of ease and excitement about buying while at the same time offering justification to rationalize this choice.

Your prospects must be open to discussion and trust. Doubts are the adversary of persuasion. Since at the beginning of a sales call, your primary function is to help a prospect speak to you and to believe what you are saying, you have to establish relationships and trust.

Subliminal persuasion is the most powerful form of report construction.

Other factors that are subliminal affect credibility.

For example, you have to know what works for you and, in particular, you have to connect your sales, the industry in which you work to optimize your impact on people.

The appropriately dressed salesperson displays an appreciation for the customers that they are meeting and gives the illusion that they take care of how they look and act.

During the sales call, your prospects assess your trust, skill, and motives.

You might be the best salesman on earth, but if your viewpoint is assumed that you're only going to make money off them, it's doubtful that you'll make a sale. Also, if you don't know well what your product is, your prospect is likely to doubt any of what you are saying.

For example, a salesperson standing before him saying in a weak voice that it would be useful for the future, somewhat meekly and with a questioning tone, is not convincing. The message is not congruent.

There are important lessons for salespeople in the above paragraphs: be aware of your product, learn the benefits it offers to its users, and be seen subliminally in your sales presentation. Your intentions can also come through readily when you deliver the bid.

There is an Australian seller who is the leading seller in her industry. She dresses impeccably, always fast and efficient, and none of her business counterparts are familiar with her industry, industry players, regulations, and goods. Therefore, she is the most popular seller in Australia, highly paid, and constantly pursued abroad in this industry.

You can improve your chances by making the viewer feel good. Some it call the law of association.

The saying "It isn't what you say, it's how you say it," is a lot of truth.

In your language, the way you use intonation and inflammation is important for what you say.

Here's an example:

In reality, though, inflection is much of the actual meaning. Look at each sentence below, each with a different word highlighted, and followed by the implicated meaning.

The phrase "I can't promise you that value" has only one meaning.

- (but perhaps someone can.)
- I can't promise you.
- (There's no way.)
- I can't promise that price to you.
- (Perhaps you will get it.)
- I can't PROMISE that price.
- I can't assure you of the price. (But I can promise somebody else.)
- (Perhaps a reasonable price.)
- I can't give you the amount.
- (but I can promise something.)
- I can't promise you the Amount.

What we emphasize is the significance of our statements, and it is a subtle process.

We have three options. When we say it, we will end the sentence with: The intonation we use when saying a sentence.

An intonation with:

- An upward expression
- Unaltered intonation of the voice
- A high/low intonation of the accent

Pick a word and say, "You want to buy this," for you. Do this for yourself.

When you repeat this phrase and say the last two words in a higher-pitched voice, it sounds like you are asking. There are languages (e.g., Italian) where, through the intonation of a sentence, you indicate you are asking questions.

Then say the sentence that holds the tone of your voice consistent. It's not different. The tone is a statement you make.

Speak the same sentence again, but say it more and more loudly, the last two words. This is command tonality, which hypnotics use well and can also be used in hypnotic sales techniques.

How is this useful in selling?

Well, when you comment, "This product is the one you want," it has very little positive impact if you utter it with a question type tonality. It sounds like you are asking a question and are not sure if it's a good product or the best one to use.

You should construct phrases carefully with a commanding tonality that defines what you want people to do. Those are called Embedded Commands and are a highly powerful method of subliminal persuasion.

For instance:

"When customers contract my business, John, all we do is to achieve results."

"Hire my company, John ... get results... now," hears your unconscious mind.

Put together enough of these sentences in a sales presentation, and the performance will significantly improve.

To subliminally carry out your bids, you can use presuppositions.

What are the premises?

The budgets are the linguistic equivalent of the assumptions which most people name.

They are already what must be considered valid for the statement to be valid or meaningful. Budgets are supposed to be taken for granted instead of clearly defined making it much harder to avoid presuppositions.

Think of what you want to recognize as a fact to use assumptions, and then create a term that assumes this.

The strength of assumptions can be immense.

Let me give you a case in point.

The discrepancy is the use of premises, "Did you find anything in our product interesting?"

And what about:

"What do you think is most interesting about our commodity?"

The first sentence above presupposes almost nothing of value. At the same time, the second sentence presupposes several things, and the reader must choose.

Persuasive Writing Techniques

Some things do not change over time, and although we have advanced a lot in technology, there are things that, as human beings, will continue to function.

In this section, I am going to talk about persuasion techniques that are highly known and that it does not matter why they will continue to work for you whenever you use them.

Do you want to convince your readers to do something or agree with your point of view?

Well, I know this is a silly question. Of course, yes.

Persuasion is generally an exercise where a win-win situation is created. You present a case that others find beneficial. They are made an offer that they cannot refuse.

It is simply a good deal or a position that makes sense to that particular person.

However, some techniques can facilitate this work and make your case a more convincing case. While this list is by no means exhaustive, these strategies are widely used as they work!

Persuasive Writing Technique 1: Repetition

Talk to someone well versed in the psychology of learning, and they will tell you that "repetition is the mother of learning." It is also essential in persuasive writing since a person cannot agree with you if he cannot follow what you are saying.

Of course, there are good and bad repetitions. To stay on the bright side, deliver your message in different ways: directly, through an example, with a story, a quote from a famous person, and once again, in the recap.

Persuasive Writing Technique 2: Why

Note the power of the word. Psychological tests have shown that people are more likely to react to an application simply because they give them a 'why' explanation ... Even if this isn't important.

When you think about it, the plan itself makes sense. Without fair justification, we do not like to be told or asked to behave. Often offer reasons to people who you want to be open to your thinking.

Persuasive Writing Technique 3: Consistency

It has been called the "troll of small minds," but consistency in our thoughts and actions is a trait of social value. We don't want it to seem inconsistent, since, rightly or wrongly, that characteristic is associated with instability and frivolity, while consistency is related to integrity and rational behavior.

Use this in your writing, getting the reader to agree with something in advance (something easy, that almost nobody can disagree with). Then rigorously assemble your case, with lots of supporting evidence, at the same time relate your endpoint to the opening stage that has already been accepted, and there you have it!

Persuasive Writing Technique 4: Social Proof

Seeking guidance from others about what to do and what to accept is one of the most powerful psychological forces in our lives. We are social beings, and we continually look at ourselves when acting, especially when we are in a new setting where we have no previous experience (imagine sitting at a very traditional banquet with ten different types of forks on one side and knives on the other — what would you do? I'm sure you would look at the closest person to see which cutlery you choose to start with.)

Persuasion techniques: The six principles of a winning speech.

The six principles of a winning speech that every manager should know.

1. Don't be in a position of authority when you speak. Be an authority.

The difference is that they will see the first one (because of who he is). The second, they will listen to him (for what he provokes). The first speaks from the pride of the position and not from the humility of the perpetual apprentice. The second makes attendees feel first and reason later, and vibrate with each articulated gesture, with each uttered word. They follow him because they see him as credible. After all, his messages spark sparks of illusion, attention, or interest.

And that is what we have to achieve when we sit down to write a speech and when we rehearse its declamation. Provoke emotional and sensory impacts that make them draw what they hear on their mental staff, and that you feel those vibrations in the depths of their hearts because depending on how we make them feel, this will motivate them to accompany us, vote for us, applaud us... remember us.

One of the most important aspects is the brevity of sentences: short, slow, patterned. As if they were headlines for the news. Because if you save your words, you save their attention. A long message is only enunciated if this is a quote or requires a literary figure.

Remember: whoever talks a lot and with an archaic language does so to hide their ignorance or confuse the audience. Avoid both purposes, or your credibility will be affected. Only if your words create value, what you say is worth it.

2. Don't be a wrapper, but a caramel. The content gives value to the continent.

A good example is the well-known sensation that we have all experienced when we see a speaker standing on a podium, and before he utters the first word, we observe how many have already bought his message (product). Like when we buy a new detergent for the suggestiveness of the messages or a juice from a striking package and attractive colors. We do not know if we will like what is inside since we have not yet tried it. But what we do know is that its exterior has already seduced us.

As with a product, it also happens to speakers. What is the reason for that sudden success, that unrepeatable salesperson aura, that intoxicating spell that makes him win our love with his mere presence? To the charism, to the pure and simple charism. They are those types of people who want to make good the phrase that AnetteBenning receives from her lover in the movie American Beauty: "To be successful, you have to project a sense of success."

Well, you must, dear manager, be that type of person. But beware because the initial perfume can start to evaporate if you do not meet a series of unwritten requirements. The listener can never perceive that behind that seductive, different, luminous, and charismatic packaging, there is something worse than a bad product: nothing — the intellectual or personal emptiness of the person speaking to them.

It turns out that they will have spent their time listening to someone who has convinced them that their product is the best when there is simply no product. Now I ask you: What are you doing at that time? How many times have you felt like this being a listener and not a speaker? How many times have you resisted the captive urge to get up and go home? How often have you waited to sing forty to the trickster of the word, to the falsifier of consciences?

How to avoid that the one who is there, in front of you, ends with that feeling, with that void (of content)? It is easy. Don't talk like you take a flower out of your jacket. Speak as if the heart were drawing that flower on your face. Speaker, not actor. This game is not about communicating much but about communicating what is correct. Words that create added value to your listeners' knowledge, interests, and motivations. That's what they were for. Don't waste their time with cliches and platitudes. Offer them techniques, methods, tools, ways, and advice that improve their professional and personal activity.

At the beginning of your speech, say who you are, what you have done and what you are going to do, and then be consistent with your words. Do not be who you are not, do not appear as what they do not expect from you; do not promise what you know that you will not fulfill. You commit yourself to future suicide for a few moments of present illusory recognition. Think about it.

Remember: when we do not shine (sincerity and knowledge) on the counterpart but only try to dazzle it (rhetorical flash), in the end, the communication space becomes a twilight zone (no credibility).

3. If you submit to the papers, in the end, you will end up losing them.

Remember this maxim when you have a public appearance, private intervention, or keynote speech. If you read, you do not connect the same, and you are not so natural or spontaneous. If you submit to the dictatorship of the folio, the base of every tree, you will end up like this: subject to its roots, immovable, insecure, and accommodated in a fictional comfort zone that, little by little, will take you away from the listener.

Paper is a good stick, perhaps the best to support your momentary imbalances with your speech presentation. It helps you find yourself, it helps you locate yourself, but it makes you walk on your own. Therefore, I advise the following system: once you have written your speech, underline in each paragraph the opening phrase and the most important concept of that paragraph, the one that gives it value. Memorize them, only that part, only that phrase, and that concept, and dedicate yourself to reading the rest over and over again.

When the time comes for the speech, your naturalness will rest because you have what you want in your mind. You can express the rest with your words without losing what you want to say. In this way, you do not force yourself to make an impossible memory effort or force the audience to see how well you read, but how little you transmit.

Reading is not easy, and not even being a good speaker makes it easy to be a good reader. And accommodating yourself in reading (before in sheets and today even in teleprompters) also accommodates your brain, memory, and therefore your ability to respect yourself. Your self-esteem will be higher if you find that you can count, relate, and communicate without the magic stick's continuous help. Use it, but never abuse it. Or you will end up losing the papers.

Remember: paper is speech. But what makes that oratory is you. If you star in the role, they will end up asking you to mail it to them, and each time you will communicate to more empty audiences. Your positioning begins by assuming that you, and no one but you, are the protagonist.

4. Your history will make History.

Dare to tell stories (personal, plausible) since the public feels identified with them, either because they sound close, or because they sound credible since they will listen more and be more in agreement with your ideas. Today good storytellers succeed. We have to look for conflict, and it builds the story. Make it simple and easy to transmit from one to the other, because therein lies the key to its virality and diffusion.

Tell something that causes or has caused you pain, laughter, guilt, something perfectly adaptable to your listeners' soul and heart. We are used to listening to stories from a young age. They are interesting, visual, let the imagination run wild, and foster powerful narrative communication. In short, they are very powerful. But they must see it (and feel it). Because if they see it, they will tell it.

5. Break patterns. Change paradigms. It provokes. Be flamboyant.

Before writing your speech, think about how you want your conclusion to be seen. As a nice, outgoing, reference speaker in his field, close, educational, entertaining, all of this at the same time. How? This panoramic HD (High Definition) will define your intervention. And if you fill it with continuous stimuli, the better. That they see something that they have never seen before, that they hear a phrase never before constructed. That they leave with the feeling that there must be a second part in their agendas to listen to you again.

Seek originality, but stay away from geeks. Innovate, but always remain attached to creativity and talent and not to spontaneous improvisation. Encourage them to emulate you. And for this, help yourself with the community symbology, that is, with those references, examples, that link, unite or bring you closer to those present so that they see you as close, accessible, and even as one of their own.

6. Tactical wins win the strategy.

Tactical victory comes when you master every part of your speech; when you know by heart the structure that will guide your steps with a firm word. That electrifying start, that 20-second connection that will make you begin to earn the respect of those present. The right moment to introduce the story, example, or anecdote is the timing domain (now I stop, now I accelerate) using the full-stop technique.

That end that is approaching and for which people were already warned by creating prior expectations. Small continuous points achieve the game, and many games allow you to win the set. In the speech, it is key to balance and control the rhythm and voice of the words, their correct intonation and speed, their exact location, and their relationship to the context you speak. There may be good arguments, sound ideas, irrefutable examples that if we do not control the rhythmic and musical pentagram, we will not convince.

We must know how to locate and identify the important idea of each paragraph of each part of our speech. And just before getting to that important idea or concepts, the corresponding pause, proper silence. With this, we will generate what I call communicative tension: create expectations with your messages. People have to perceive that what comes next in your speech exceeds what they have already heard. The speaker should be the thermostat of the speech: controlling the rhythm to pause and guide your messages and regulating the voice to define them.

Remember: Never scream or speak too loud. Where ideas do not reach, your voice should not reach because the tone of the message is the spirit of the idea.

CHAPTER 5

METHODS OF MASS MEDIA INFLUENCE ON THE SUBCONSCIOUS

Mass media is the most effective weapon for mass exploitation used by the capitalist class. They form and describe natural, reasonable attitudes and opinions. This chapter explores the activities of mass media to explain their true position in society through the ideas of the main thinkers, the mechanism of power and strategies they employ.

Some of the theories in this chapter speak about the supernatural symmetry found in popular culture objects. Many valid questions emerge from such a theory about the meaning of such symbols and the people who put them here. But without considering many other items, I cannot provide satisfactory answers to these questions.

Programming Via Mass Media

Mass media are forms of media designed to reach the widest possible audience. These include TV, film, radio, magazines, books, songs, games, the internet, and video games. In the past century, numerous studies have been carried out to measure the impact of mass media on the population to identify the best techniques for influencing them. From these studies emerged the science of communications used in marketing, public relations, and politics: mass communication is a necessary tool for the functioning of a vast democracy; it is also a necessary tool for a dictatorship. It all depends on its use.

In the preface to his 1958 Best of the Worlds, Aldous Huxley paints a rather somber portrait of society. He believes that an "impersonal force controls it," a ruling elite that manipulates the population through various methods.

The impersonal forces over which we had almost no control seem to all push us towards the Best-worldly nightmare; and this impersonal push is being knowingly accelerated by representatives of political and commercial organizations which have developed several techniques to manipulate, in the interest of a certain minority, the thoughts and feelings of the masses.

His dark perspective is not just a mere hypothesis or an illusion of paranoia. It is a certified fact, present in the most important world studies on mass media. Here are a few:

ELITE THINKERS

WALTER LIPPMANN

The American intellectual Walter Lippmann was one of the first works on mass media use and was awarded the Pulitzer Prize two times. Lippmann compares mass in public opinion (1922) with a "big beast" and a "perplexed flock," which was to be led by a ruling class. He described the governing elite as a "specialized class with a vast diversity of interests beyond the local community." According to Lippmann, the experts who often have called themselves "the Elite" will soon be a system of intelligence that circumvents the key democratic shortcomings, representing the impossible dream of an "all-powerful citizen." "Puzzled herd" has its function to roar and trample, to be "the disinterested spectator of the event," not a participant. The "responsible person," who is not an ordinary citizen, is obliged to participate.

Thus, mass media and propaganda are instruments which must be used without physical correction by the elite to direct the public. The 'fabrication of consent,' in other words, manipulating the public opinion to embrace the elite's plan is an important idea put forth in Lippmann. The general public can not reason and determine important issues in Lippmann's view. So the elite will decide "for their own sake," and then sell the decisions to the masses.

I think no one denies that this manufacture of consent can make major improvements. The mechanism by which public opinion is formed is certainly no less nuanced than its pages and the possibilities for exploitation, which are fairly obvious for anyone who understands the method... The practice of democracy has changed as a result of psychological research combined with modern communication means. The influence of propaganda, not necessarily in the pejorative sense of the term, has made the old conservatives of our thought unpredictable. The change takes place that is more important than all the variations in the economy... For example, the original democracy dogma cannot be taken for granted; the human heart naturally derives the intelligence required to handle human affairs. If you act on this theory, you expose yourself to frustration and forms of belief that you can not verify. We are proving to do nothing to deal with the world beyond our grasp with intuition, awareness, or accidents of hasty opinion.

It is worth noting that Lippmann is one of the founding fathers of the CFR, the world's most influential think tank for foreign policy. It must give you some insight into the elite's state of mind in the use of the media.

In the United States, political and economic influence is centralized within a "ruling class," which is in the hands of the majority of foreign businesses, the mass media, the most powerful foundations, private universities, and most public services in the United States. The Foreign Relations Board was established in 1921 and is the key connection between large companies and the federal administration. This was called the 'school of state people' and something like an organ of what C. Wright Mills called the Power Elite — a group of people who have the same interests and the same ways of thinking that shape events from the background the invulnerable.

The new CFR Members include David Rockefeller, Dick Cheney, Barack Obama, Hilary Clinton, Rick Warren, and leading companies, including CBS, Nike, Coca-Cola, and Visa. Other new CFR members include:

CARL JUNG

Carl Jung is the pioneer of analytical psychology and discusses the mind's comprehension through vision, poetry, mythology, religion, symbolism, and philosophy. At the root of many psychological concepts, such as archetype, complexity, individual, introvert/extravert, and synchronicity, is the Swiss therapist. The hidden environment of his family greatly influenced him. A fervent Freemason, his grandfather, Carl Gustav, was the great Master, and the Rosicrucians were found out by Jung himself. It could explain the great interest he had in the philosophy of the West and the East, Alchemy, Astrology, and Symbolism.

There is a second psychological structure of a collective, universal and impersonal type, identical with all individuals, as well as our immediate, truly personal consciousness, which we believe is the only empirical psyche (even if we insert the personal unconscious in the appendix). We do not grow this collective unconscious individually but by heritage. It consists of pre-existing forms, the archetypes that can only be secondarily recognized, and offer that psychic material a defined form.

In various civilizations, the collective unconscious emerges by the presence of identical images and mythological characters. The archetylistic symbols seem to have been integrated into our collective subconscious, and we exhibit a natural curiosity and appeal when we are exposed. Therefore, occult symbols may have a significant impact on people, even if many people never directly are confronted with the mystical meaning of the symbol. This concept has been found by mass media thinkers like Edward D. Bernays to manipulate the public's collective and personal subconscious.

EDWARD BERNAYS

The "Public Relations man," Edward Bernays, uses techniques that his uncle Sigmund Freud invented to influence public opinion using the Unconscious. He shared the dream of Walter Lippmann for the population as irrational and subject to the "herd revolution."

Conscious and intelligent manipulation of organized mass habits and views is a key element in a democratic society. An invisible government that powers the country is the one who manipulates this invisible system of society.

We are governed, our minds are created, our preferences are influenced, and our ideas are suggested, mostly by people we never heard of. The way our democratic society is structured is a logical result. Many people have to work together this way if they want to stay together again in a trouble-free community.

In certain cases, our unseen rulers are unaware of their colleagues' presence in the closed circle.

The way American society works has dramatically changed creative marketing strategies by Barneys. He generated "consumerism" literally by developing a society where Americans shop for pleasure rather than survive. That's why Life Magazine is considered one of the Top 100 of 20th-century prominent Americans.

HAROLD LASSWELL

In 1939-1940, the University of Chicago hosted a series of

secret communications seminars. These think tanks were funded by the Rockefeller Foundation and included the most important researchers in communication and sociological studies. One of his scholars was Harold Lasswell, a leading political scientist and communications theorist specializing in the analysis of propaganda. He also shared that democracy, a people-led government, could not be sustained without a specialized elite that shaped public opinion through propaganda.

In his Encyclopedia of Social Sciences, Lasswell explains that when the elites lack the strength required for forced obedience, social managers must turn to "a whole new technique of control, largely through propaganda." He added the conventional justification to it: "ignorance and stupidity [of] ... the masses and not succumb to democratic dogmatisms that men are the best judges of their interests."

Lasswell has studied the area of content analysis extensively to understand the effectiveness of different types of propaganda. In his essay, The Contents of Communication, Lasswell explains that, to understand the meaning of a message (i.e., a book, a speech, a film, etc.), the frequency of use of such symbols in the message, the way these symbols serve to influence the viewers' views and the strength of the symbols used must be considered.

Lasswell was famous for his media analysis based on this:

"Who (says) What (to) Who (through) What Means (with) What Effect."

Using this model, Lasswell indicates that to analyze a media product properly, we need to look at who produced it (the people who ordered it), for whom it is intended (the target audience) and what are the desired effects of the product (inform, convince, sell, etc.) on the audience.

Here's the review of a Rihanna video: WHO PRODUCED: Vivendi Universal; Whom: Rihanna's pop artist; TO WHOM: consumers aged 9-25; WHAT MEANS: the clip; and WHAT EFFECT: the seller: its music, its image, and its message.

The study of films and videos on The Vigilant Citizen gives the message that has been conveyed to the considerable public significance. The word "Illuminati" is sometimes used to describe a select group of leaders who secretly rule the masses. Though the word may sound very caricatured and conspiratory, it accurately represents the elite closeness of secret societies and occult knowledge. Yet I refuse to explain what is happening in the mass media using the word "conspiracy theory." Could we still call this "conspiracy theory" because all the details about the industry's elitist character are publicly available?

Throughout popular culture, there were many different beliefs, thoughts, and opinions. But the convergence of media companies has culminated in the entertainment sector being consolidated. Have you ever wondered why all new music sounds the same, and all new movies look the same? In the following section, the answer can be found:

Media Ownership

A list of properties managed with AOL Time Warner is

contained in ten pages listing 292 separate companies and subsidiaries. Twenty-two of them are joint ventures with different stages of media operations. These partners include 3Com, E-Bay (American Express, Homestore, Sony, Viva, Bertelsmann, and Polygram), and Hewlett-Packard (Cities Group, Citygroup). AOL Time Warner's most familiar properties: Book of the Monday Club: Little Brown Publishers, HBO and its seven networks, CNN, seven international and specialty networks, Beep beep, vil coyote studios, Popular science, and 52 other record labels. -- "New Media Monopoly," Ben Bagdikan.

Warner's AOL Time:

-- 64 ratings, among them TIME, LIFE, People, MAD, DC comics.

-- Film features for Warner Bros, New Line, and Fine Line.

-- More than 40 labels, with Warner Bros, Atlantic and Electra included.

-- Various networks of television, such as Network AB, HBO, Cinemax, TNT, Cartoon Network, CNN.

Viacom has the following:

CBS, MTV, MTV2, UPN, VH1, Showtime, Nickelodeon, Central Comedy, TNN, CMT, BET

-- Nickelodeon films, MTV films, Paramount images

-- Videos from Blockbuster

-- 1800 film displays by famous players

Disney has a hockey team called the Anaheim Mighty

Ducks, which is no longer adequate to reflect the Empire's vastness. Hollywood continues to be the icon and has eight production studios and dealers: Walt Disney Pictures, Hollywood Pictures, and Caravan Pictures.

ABC Television Network with its ten networks, in the Top five of its activities on the market; 30 radio stations, including all the largest on the market; 11 cable outlets, including Disney and ESPN (jointly), A&E and the history channel; 13 internal outlets, including Disney and ESPN (jointly) CASS, manages eight publishing houses of Walt Disney and ABC Publishing Books.

-- Ibid.-Ibid.

The corporation owns Walt Disney:

-- ABC, ESPN, A&E, ESPN, Web of History.

-- Walt Disney Images, Hollywood Pictures, and Aspect of the Miramax Film Corp.

-- Hannah Montana, Miley Cyrus, and Jonas Brothers. Montana and Selena Gomez.

Universal Vivendi has the following:

-- 27% of the US sales of music, including Interscope, Geffen, A&M, Island, Def Jam, MCA, Mercury, Motown, and Universal

-- Universal Studios, Channel studio, Polygram Films.

-- A lot of Internet and telecommunications companies,

-- Lady Gaga, Lil Wayne, Mariah Spears, Mariah Carey, Lil Gaga, The Black Eyed Peas.

Sony controls the following:

-- Columbia photos, gems, classical Sony photos

-- 15% of music sales in the US: Columbia, Epic, Sony, Arista, Jive and RCA Records

-- Michael Jackson, Alicia Keys, Christina Aguilera, Beyonce, Shakira,

A few cultural actors represent a limited number of views and ideas that are open to the public.

It means, too, that an idea can quickly saturate all media platforms to agree (such as "mass destruction weapons in Iraq").

The Standardization Of Human Thought

A global oligarchy of media conglomerates has been formed through the merger of media companies in recent decades. FIVE companies are making the TV shows, the songs that we listen to, the films we watch, and the newspapers that we read. The members of these organizations are closely linked to the global elite and are the elite in several respects. Such conglomerates have the power to build a common and consistent view of the future that promotes "standardization of the human imagination" by providing all those channels that can touch the masses.

Even the movements and styles considered marginal are, in fact, extensions of the main thought. The mass media produce their rebels who seem to be part of it and continue to be part of the established order and challenge it. Artists, creations, and ideas that do not correspond to the main way of thinking are forgotten and mercilessly rejected by the conglomerates, making them virtually disappear from society itself. However, ideas that are considered valid and desirable to be accepted by society are skillfully marketed to the masses to turn them into self-evident standards.

In 1928, Edward Barneys had already seen the immense potential of cinema to standardize thoughts:

American cinema is the largest subconscious carrier of propaganda in the world today. It is a great distributor of ideas and opinions. The cinema can standardize the ideas and habits of a nation. Because images are made to meet market demands, they reflect, emphasize, and even exaggerate popular trends, rather than stimulating new ideas and opinions. The cinema uses ideas and facts that are in vogue. While the newspapers seek to provide the facts, it [the cinema] seeks to provide entertainment.

In the 1930s, Frankfurt school thinkers like Theodor Adorno and Herbert Marcuse marked these facts as a threat to human freedom. Three key issues with the cultural industry were identified. Branching can:

1. Reduce people to "population status" by hindering the creation of self-employed persons who can determine rationally.

2. Replace the valid dynamism of individuality and self-visibility with the tranquility of conformism and passivity.

3. Validate the belief that people are trying to escape the insane and cruel world they live in by hypnotically losing themselves.

The notion of escape is even more relevant today with the advent of online video games, 3D movies, and home theaters. The masses, seeking state-of-the-art entertainment, will resort to big-budget products that can only be produced by the world's largest media corporations. These products contain deliberately placed messages and symbols that are nothing more than entertaining propaganda. The public has been trained to LIKE this propaganda, to the point of spending their hard-earned money to be exposed to it.

About propaganda, the early defenders of universal literacy and the free press considered two possibilities: propaganda may be true, or it may be false. They did not foresee what happened, especially in our western capitalist democracies — the development of a vast mass consumer industry, concerned in absolute terms neither with the true nor with the false, but more or less irrelevant with the unreal. In a term, the almost limitless human appetite for diversion was not taken into consideration.

A single medium also has no enduring impact on the psychology of humans. However, the mass media creates a living environment in which we evolve every day because of their omnipresent nature. The norm is defined, and the unwanted excluded. Likewise, when wearing the blinds, the masses can only see where they are supposed to see so that they can only see what is before them.

The emergence of the mass media makes the use of propaganda techniques on a societal scale. The orchestration of the press, radio, and television to create a continuous, lasting, and total environment makes the influence of propaganda virtually unsuspected precisely because it creates a constant environment. Mass media provides the essential link between the individual and the demands of the technological society.

One of the reasons why the mass media successfully influences industrial society is due to the considerable amount of research on cognitive sciences and human nature that has been applied to it...

Handling techniques

Advertising is a deliberate attempt to control the public's perception of a subject. Advertising topics include people (for example politicians or playing artists), goods and services, organizations of all types, works of art and entertainment.

The effort to sell products and ideas to the masses has led to an unprecedented amount of research on human behavior and the human psyche. Cognitive science, psychology, sociology, semiotics, linguistics, and other related fields were still greatly sought after by well-funded studies.

No group of sociologists can approach advertising teams about the collection and processing of social data. Advertising teams have billions per year to spend on research and reaction testing, and their products are magnificent accumulations of substance regarding the feelings and experiences of the entire community.

These studies' results are applied to advertisements, films, clips, and other media to make them as influential as possible. The art of marketing is highly scientific and calculated because it must reach both the collective and the individual unconscious. As far as the big-budget goods are concerned, a video is never "just a video." To achieve the desired effect, images, symbols, and meanings are put strategically.

It is also with the knowledge of the human being, his tendencies, desires, needs, psychic mechanism, and automatisms as that of social psychology and analytical psychology that propaganda can refine his techniques.

Propaganda today hardly ever uses logical or rational arguments. It will directly draw on the most basic human needs and instincts to generate an emotional and irrational response. If we thought rationally, likely, we would not buy 50% of what we have.

Sex is ubiquitous in mass media since it attracts and keeps the viewer's attention. This immediately puts itself in communication with our instinct to perpetuate the species, to reproduce us. When it is triggered, this instinct can overshadow any other rational thought in our brain.

Subliminal Perception

What if the messages mentioned above could reach the audience without even knowing what is happening? What if? This is the purpose of subliminal perception. In 1957 US market researcher James Vicary coined the word 'subliminal advertising,' which claimed that anyone who went to the films could drink 'Coca-Cola' and 'eat popcorn.' The presentation of these messages is brief enough for the spectator to be unaware of.

Subliminal awareness is a deliberate process produced by communication technicians that allows you to receive and address information and instructions without understanding it.

This technique is frequently used in commercialization, and we all know that sex sells.

Although some sources claim that subliminal publicity is ineffective or even an urban legend, the documented application of this technique in mass media shows that its designers believe in its power. The efficacy of recent studies has also been demonstrated, particularly when the message is negative.

"To instill negative thinking, a team at University College London, funded by the Wellcome Trust, found that it was especially good." "There has been a lot of speculation about whether people can interact with emotional information, including pictures, faces, and words in a subconscious way," said Professor Nill Lavie. "We have demonstrated that people can understand the emotional meaning of subliminal messages and have shown that people are much more in line with bad words.

Desensitization

In the past, when people were subject to changes, they took to the streets, protested, even triggered riots. The main reason for these clashes was because the changes were clearly announced by the leaders and understood by the population. It was sudden, and the effects could be analyzed and assessed. Today, when the elite needs the public to understand part of their plan, they do so through desensitization. The program, which may go against the best interests of the public, is slowly, gradually and repeatedly presented to the world through films (by involving it in the plot) clips (which make it cool and sexy) or the news (which presents it as a solution to current problems). After several years of mass exposure to a particular program, the elite openly exposes its project to the world. Because of mental programming, it is greeted with general indifference and passively accepted. This technique comes from psychotherapy.

These psychotherapy techniques, widely practiced and accepted as a means of curing psychological disorders, are also methods of controlling people. They can be systematically used to influence attitudes and behaviors. Systematic desensitization is used to alleviate anxiousness to ensure that a specific fear of violence, for example, no longer perturbs the patient (the public). [...] If they are exposed to them enough, people respond to terrifying circumstances.

You can often find predictive programming in the science fiction genre. It represents a specific image of the future — the one desired by the elite — which ultimately becomes inevitable in men's minds. Ten years ago, the public was desensitized to the war against the Arab world. Today, the public is gradually exposed to the existence of mind control, transhumanism, and the existence of an Illuminati elite. Emerging from the shadows, these concepts are now everywhere in popular culture. This is what Alice Bailey describes under the name "outsourcing of the hierarchy": those who lead in the shadows reveal themselves slowly ...

Occult Symbolism In Popular Culture

Metropolis - An elite film for the elite?

Documentation on occult symbolism is rather difficult to find. This should not be surprising since the term "occult" literally means "hidden." It also means "reserved for those who know" since it is only communicated to those who are considered worthy of this knowledge. It is neither taught in schools nor discussed by the media. It is therefore considered marginal or even ridiculous by the general population.

Occult knowledge in occult circles, however, is NOT seen as absurd. It's considered eternal and sacred. There is a long history of hermeneutic and supernatural knowledge, taught by secret societies from Ancient Egypt, the Mystics of Eastern Europe, the Templar kings, and modern Freemasons. Even if nature and the extent of this knowledge have most probably been modified, altered through the centuries, the schools of the occult have kept their main characteristics, which are highly symbolic, ceremonial, and metaphysical. These characteristics, which were a complex part of ancient civilizations, have been completely removed from modern society to be replaced by a materialist pragmatism. Thus, there is a large gap in understanding between the average person and the ritualist institution.

If this esoteric doctrine has always been hidden from the masses, for whom a simpler code has been partitioned, is it not highly probable that the representatives of every aspect of modern civilization — philosophical, ethical and scientific — are ignorant of the true meaning of these very theories and principles on which their beliefs are based? That hiding behind their beautiful façade are the arts and sciences which the race has inherited from older nations, a mystery that only the most enlightened intellectuals can understand? Surely that's the case.

The "simpler code" partitioned for the masses used to be organized religions. It has become the Temple of Mass Media and daily preaches extreme materialism, spiritual emptiness, and an individualistic, self-directed existence. It is exactly the opposite of the attributes required to become a truly free man, as taught by the great schools of thought. Is a stupid population easier to deceive and manipulate?

These blind slaves are told that they are "free" and "well educated," even when they walk behind the signs that would make them flee from panicking and shouting any peasant of the Middle Ages. The sign on the sign will be similar to the symbols that Modern Man accepts in the naive faith of a child: "Direct your death and slavery," as a peasant of antiquity would understand.

This chapter examines the leading thinkers in mass media, the structure of media influence, and the techniques employed for mass manipulation. I think it is important to consider "why" in matters on The Vigilant Citizen that are discussed. The dichotomy that is portrayed in many articles between the "population base" and "ruling class" is not a "construction theory," but is a fact that has been accurately articulated in the work of some of the most important men of the twentieth century.

Lippmann, Lasswell, and Bernays all said that it is difficult for the public to determine its fate, which is the goal of democracy. Their thoughts continue to apply to societies. It is becoming increasingly clear that an ignorant population is not an obstacle that the leaders have to face; it's something DESIRABLE, and indeed necessary to ensure complete leadership. Their idea is always being applied to society, but a hidden regime, a ruling class in charge of the puzzle. An ignorant community is not searching for its rights, and it is not trying to obtain a better understanding and authority of the problems. It just goes along with the pattern. Popular culture provides and nurtures ignorance by constantly serving as entertainment for the brain and bringing degenerate celebrities to worship.

This hopes for what has never been and will never be if it wishes to be naive and free.

CHAPTER 6

PSYCHOLOGICAL METHODS OF MANIPULATING THE MENTAL CONSCIOUSNESS OF MAN AND THE MASSES

Consider the psychological techniques of manipulating the mental consciousness of man and the masses. For convenience, we divide the proposed methods into eight blocks, effective both individually and together.

The life of any person is multifaceted by the life experience that this person has, by the level of education, by the genetic component, by many other factors that must be taken into account for the psychological impact on the person. Specialists in manipulating the psyche (psychotherapists, hypnologists, criminal hypnotists, fraudsters, government officials, etc.) use different technologies to control people. It is necessary to know such methods, including and to counter this kind of manipulation. Knowledge is power. It is knowledge about the mechanisms of manipulation of the human psyche that allows you to resist illegal intrusions into the psyche (into the subconscious of a person) and, therefore, protect yourself.

It should be noted that there are a large number of methods of psychological impact (manipulation). Some of

85

them are available for mastering only after a long practice (for example, NLP), some are freely used by most people in life, sometimes without even noticing it; it is enough to have ideas about some methods of manipulative influence to defend oneself already; to counteract others, you need to have a good command of such techniques (for example, gypsy psychological hypnosis), etc. To the extent that such a step is permissible, we will reveal the secrets of controlling the mental consciousness of a person and the masses (collective, assembly, audience, crowd, etc.).

It is worth noting that only recently has the opportunity appeared to talk about early secret techniques openly. At the same time, such tacit permission from the oversight bodies is quite justified, since we are convinced that a certain part of the truth is revealed to a person only at a certain stage. Collecting such material bit by bit — a person is formed into the desired person. If for some reason, a person is still ready to comprehend the truth, fate itself will lead him aside. And if such a person even finds out about some secret techniques, then he will not be able to realize their significance. That is, this kind of information will not find the necessary response in his soul, and in his psyche, a stupor will turn on, thanks to which such information will simply not be perceived by the brain, i.e., will not be remembered by such a person.

Below we will consider the manipulation techniques outlined by blocks of equivalent ineffectiveness. Even though its inherent name precedes each block, nevertheless, it should be noted that the specifics of methods of influencing the subconscious are very effective for all, without exception, regardless of the specific target audience or typical personality characteristics of a person. This is explained by the fact that the human psyche has common components and differs only in insignificant details, hence the increased efficiency of the developed manipulation techniques in the world.

- The first block of manipulation techniques

Methods Of Manipulating The Human Mental Consciousness

1. False interrogation, or deceptive clarifications

In this case, the manipulative effect is achieved because the manipulator pretends that he wants to better understand something for himself, asks you again, but repeats your words only at the beginning and then only partially, introducing a different meaning into the meaning of what you said earlier, thereby changing the general meaning of what was said to please yourself.

In this case, you should be extremely careful, always listen to what you are being told about, and noticing a catch — clarify what you said earlier; moreover, to clarify even if the manipulator, pretending not to notice your desire for clarification, tries to move on to another topic.

2. Deliberate haste, or leaping to a new topic

The manipulator in this case, after voicing any information, seeks to quickly switch to another topic, realizing that your attention will immediately be redirected to new information, which increases the likelihood that previous information that has not been "protested" will reach the subconscious listener; if the information reaches the subconscious, it is known that after any information is in the unconscious (subconscious), after a while, it is realized by a person, i.e., passes into consciousness. Moreover, if the manipulator additionally strengthened his information with an emotional load, or even introduced it into the subconscious by the encoding method, then such information will appear at the moment necessary for the manipulator, which he will provoke (for example, using the principle of "anchoring" from NLP, or, in other words, by activating the code).

Also, as a result of haste and skipping topics, it becomes possible for a relatively short period to "voice" a large number of topics; which means that censorship of the psyche will not have time to let everything through it, and the likelihood that a certain part of the information will penetrate the subconscious mind will increase. From there, it will affect the manipulated object's consciousness in a way that is beneficial to the manipulator.

3. The desire to show their indifference or pseudo-carelessness

In this case, the manipulator tries to perceive both the interlocutor and the information received as indifferently as possible, thereby unconsciously making the person try to convince the manipulator of its significance for him at all costs. Thus, the manipulator can only control the information emanating from the object of its manipulations, obtaining those facts that the object was not going to spread before. A similar circumstance on the part of the person to whom the manipulation is directed is laid down in the laws of the psyche, forcing any person to strive at all costs to prove his case by convincing the manipulator (not suspecting that he is a manipulator), and using the existing arsenal of logical controllability of thoughts — that is, the presentation of new circumstances of the case, facts that, in his opinion, can help him in this.

In this case, it is recommended to strengthen their voluntary control and not succumb to provocations as a counteraction.

4. False inferiority, or imaginary weakness

This principle of manipulation is aimed at the desire on the part of the manipulator to show his weakness to the object of manipulation, and thereby achieve the desired result because if someone is weaker, the indulgence effect is turned on, which means that censorship of the human psyche begins to function in a relaxed mode, as if not perceiving what is coming from manipulator information in earnest. Thus, the information coming from the manipulator passes immediately to the subconscious, is stored there in the form of attitudes and behavior patterns, which means that the manipulator reaches his goal, because the manipulation object itself, without suspecting it, will begin to execute the settings laid down in the subconscious, or, in other words, to execute the secret will of the manipulator.

The main method of confrontation is the complete control of information coming from any person, i.e., any person is an adversary, and he must be taken seriously.

5. False love, or the euthanasia of vigilance

Because one individual (manipulator) plays love, excessive respect, reverence, etc. in front of another (manipulation object) (i.e., expresses his feelings in a similar vein), he achieves incomparably more than if he openly asked for something.

In order not to succumb to such provocations, you should have a "cold mind."

6. Violent pressure, or exorbitant anger

In this case, manipulation becomes possible as a result of unmotivated rage on the part of the manipulator. The person to whom this kind of manipulation is directed will have a desire to calm someone angry with him. Why is he subconsciously ready to make concessions to the manipulator?

Countermeasures can be different, depending on the skills of the object of manipulation. For example, as a result of "tuning" (the so-called calibration in NLP), one can first stage a state of mind similar to a manipulator, and after calming down, calm the manipulator as well. Or, for example, you can show your calmness and absolute indifference to the anger of the manipulator, thereby confusing him, which means depriving him of his manipulative advantage. You can sharply speed up your aggressiveness with speech techniques at the same time as a light touch of the manipulator (his hand, shoulder, arm...), and additional visual impact. That is, in this case, we seize the initiative, and with the help of the simultaneous impact on the manipulator with the help of visual, auditory and kinesthetic stimuli — we introduce him into a state of trance. This means he depends on you, because in this state the manipulator himself becomes the object of our influence, and we can introduce certain settings into his subconscious because it is known that in a state of anger, any person is subject to coding (psychoprogramming). You can use other methods of counteraction. It should be remembered that in a state of anger, a person is easier to make laugh. You should know about this feature of the psyche and use it in time.

7. Fast pace, or unjustified rush

In this case, we should talk about the manipulator's desire due to the imposed excessively fast pace of speech to push some ideas, having achieved approval by their object of manipulation. This becomes possible even when the manipulator, hiding behind the alleged lack of time, achieves an incomparably greater amount from the manipulation object than if this happened over a long period, during which the manipulation object would have time to ponder his answer, and therefore not become a victim of deception (manipulation).

In this case, you should take a timeout (refer to an urgent phone call, etc.) to bring down the manipulator at a given tempo. To do this, you can play the misunderstanding of some questions and "stupid" interrogation, etc.

8. Excessive suspicion, or evoking forced excuses

A similar type of manipulation occurs when the manipulator plays suspicion in any issue. As a response to suspicion, the object of manipulation follows a desire to justify himself. Thus, his psyche's protective barrier is weakening, which means that the manipulator is achieving his goal, "pushing" the necessary psychological attitudes into his subconscious.

A defense option is to recognize yourself as a person and to resist any attempt at any manipulative influence on your psyche (i.e., you must demonstrate your self-confidence and show that if the manipulator is suddenly offended, then let him be offended, and if he wants to leave, you don't run after him; this should be adopted by "lovers": do not let yourself be manipulated.)

9. Imaginary fatigue, or a game of consolation

With all his appearance, the manipulator shows fatigue and the inability to prove something and listen to any objections. Thus, the object of manipulation tries to quickly agree with the words given by the manipulator, so as not to bore him with his objections. Well, agreeing, he thereby goes on about the manipulator, who only needs it.

One way to counter this is to not succumb to provocations.

10. The credibility of the manipulator, or deception of power

This manipulation proceeds from such specifics of the individual psyche as the worship of authorities in any field.

Most often, it turns out that the very area in which such an "authority" has achieved a result lies in a completely different sphere than its imaginary "request" now. Still, the object of manipulation cannot do anything about it, since in the soul, most people believe that there is always someone who has achieved more than them.

A variant of the confrontation is faith in one's exclusiveness, super personality, the development in yourself of the belief in your chosenness, that you are a super-person.

11. Courtesy, or help fee

The manipulator informs the object of manipulation conspiratorially about something as if advising him to decide in a friendly manner. At the same time, hiding behind an imaginary friendship (in fact, they may be familiar for the first time), as a tip, inclines the object of manipulation to the variant of solution that is primarily needed by the manipulator.

You need to believe in yourself and remember that you have to pay for everything. And it's better to pay right away, i.e., before you are required to pay a fee in the form of gratitude for the service provided.

12. Resistance, or protest

In some words, a manipulator excites feelings in the soul of the object of manipulation, aimed at overcoming the barrier (censorship of the psyche) that has arisen, to achieve his goal. It is known that the psyche is structured in such a way that a person wants to a greater extent what is forbidden to him or what efforts must be made to achieve.

Whereas that which may be better and more important, but lies on the surface, is often overlooked.

Confidence and will, i.e., you should always rely only on yourself, and not give in to weaknesses.

13. Factor particular, or from details to error

The manipulator forces the object of manipulation to pay attention to only one specific detail, not allowing him to notice the main thing. Based on this, he draws the appropriate conclusions, accepted by the consciousness of it as an uncontested basis of the meaning of what was said. It should be noted that this is very common in life when most people allow themselves to make their own opinions about a subject, without actually having any facts or more detailed information, and often without having their own opinions about what they judge using the opinions of others. Therefore, such an opinion is possible to impose on them, which means manipulating them to achieve their goal.

To counter, it is necessary to constantly work on yourself to increase your knowledge and education level.

14. The irony, or the manipulation of a grin

Manipulation is achieved because the manipulator chooses an initially ironic tone as if unconsciously calling into question any words of the object of manipulation. In this case, the object of manipulation is much faster "losing his temper"; and since anger makes critical thinking more difficult, a person enters into ASCs (altered states of consciousness), in which consciousness easily passes early forbidden information through it.

For effective protection, you should show your complete indifference to the manipulator. The feeling of being a super-person, "chosen," will help you to be condescending to the attempt to manipulate you — as to children's fun. The manipulator will immediately feel this condition intuitively, because the manipulators usually have well-developed sense organs, which, we note, allows them to feel the right moment for carrying out their manipulative techniques.

15. Interruption, or departure of thoughts

The manipulator achieves his goal by constantly interrupting the thought of the object of manipulation, directing the topic of conversation necessary for the manipulator.

As a counteraction, you can ignore the interruptions of the manipulator, or use special speech psychotechnics to make fun of him among the audience. If you laugh at a person, all his subsequent words are no longer taken seriously.

16. Provoking imaginary, or far-fetched accusations

Such manipulations become possible as a result of communicating to the object of manipulation the information that can cause him anger, and therefore reduce the criticality in assessing the alleged information. After this, such a person is broken for a certain period, during which the manipulator achieves the imposition of his will.

Protection - believe in yourself and not pay attention to others.

17. Trapping, or imaginary recognition of the opponent's gain

In this case, the manipulator, while carrying out the act of manipulation, hints at more favorable conditions in which the opponent (the object of manipulation) is supposedly located, thereby forcing the latter to make excuses in every possible way, and become open to manipulations that usually follow the manipulator.

Protection is self-awareness as a super-personality, which means a completely reasonable "elevation" over the manipulator, especially if he considers himself "insignificant." Therefore, faith in yourself and faith in your exceptionalism will help overcome any traps on the way to your consciousness from the side of manipulators.

18. Cheating in the palm of your hand, or imitation of bias

The manipulator intends to place the object of manipulation in certain predetermined conditions. The person selected as the object of manipulation, trying to avert his suspicion of excessive bias towards the manipulator, allows manipulation to take place due to the unconscious conviction of the good intentions of the manipulator. That is, he seems to be giving himself the option not to react critically to the manipulator's words, thereby unconsciously allowing the words of the manipulator to pass into his consciousness.

19. Intentional misconception, or specific terminology

In this case, the manipulation is carried out through the use of the manipulator of specific terms that are not clear to the object of manipulation. The latter, because of the danger of seeming illiterate, lacks the courage to clarify what these terms mean.

The way to counter this is to ask and clarify something incomprehensible to you.

20. The imposition of false stupidity, or through humiliation to victory

The manipulator seeks in every way to reduce the role of the object of manipulation, hinting at his stupidity and illiteracy, to thus destabilize the positive mindset of the object of manipulation, plunge his psyche into a state of chaos and temporary confusion, and thus achieve his will over him through verbal manipulation and (or) coding the psyche.

Protection - do not pay attention. It is generally recommended to pay less attention to the meaning of the words of the manipulator, and more to the details around, gestures and facial expressions, or even pretend that you are listening, and think "about your own," especially if you have an experienced fraudster or criminal hypnotist.

21. Repeatability of phrases, or the imposition of thoughts

In this type of manipulation, due to repeated phrases, the manipulator accustoms the object of manipulation to any information that is going to convey to him.

Protective installation - do not fix attention on the words of the manipulator, listen to it "in the ear," or use special speech techniques to transfer the conversation to another topic, or seize the initiative and enter the settings you need into the subconscious of the interlocutor-manipulator yourself, or many other options.

22. Erroneous speculation, or lack of understanding involuntarily

In this case, the manipulations achieve their effect due to:

- Deliberate lack of understanding by the manipulator.
- Erroneous speculation of the object of manipulation.

Moreover, even if a fraud is detected, the object of manipulation gives the impression of his guilt because he did not understand it or did not hear something.

Protection - exceptional self-confidence, the education of super-will, the formation of "chosenness" and super-personality.

23. Imaginary inattention

In this situation, the object of manipulation falls into the trap of the manipulator, playing on his own supposed inattention, so that, having achieved his own, refers to the fact that he allegedly did not notice (hear) the protest from the opponent. As a result, a manipulator puts the object of manipulation before the fact of the perfect.

Protection - clearly clarify the meaning of "agreements reached."

24. Say yes, or the path to agreement

Manipulations of this kind are carried out because the manipulator seeks to build a dialogue with the object of manipulation to always agree with his words. Thus, the manipulator skillfully brings the object of manipulation to pushing his idea, and therefore the implementation of manipulation on him.

Protection - to bring down the direction of the conversation.

25. Unexpected quotation, or the words of the opponent as evidence

In this case, the manipulative effect is achieved by unexpected quoting by the manipulator, the previously spoken words of the opponent. Such a technique acts discouragingly on the selected object of manipulation, helping the manipulator to achieve a result. Moreover, in most cases, the words themselves can be partially invented, i.e., to have a different meaning than the object of manipulation said earlier on this issue. Because the words of the object of manipulation can be simply invented, or have an only slight similarity.

Protection - also apply the method of false citation, choosing, in this case, the allegedly spoken words of the manipulator.

26. The effect of observation, or the search for similarities

As a result of preliminary observation of the manipulation object (including during the dialogue), the manipulator finds or invents any similarities between himself and the object, gently draws the attention of the object to this similarity, and thereby partially weakens the protective functions of the psyche of the manipulated object, after which he pushes his idea.

Protection - sharply emphasize in words your dissimilarity to the interlocutor-manipulator.

27. The imposition of choice, or initially the right decision

In this case, the manipulator asks the question in such a way that he does not leave the object of manipulation the possibility of making a choice other than the one voiced by the manipulator. (For example, would you like to do this or this? In this case, the keyword is "do," while initially the object of manipulation probably was not going to do anything. But he was not left with the right to choose but to choose between the first and second.)

Protection - do not pay attention, take control of any situation.

28. Unexpected revelation, or sudden honesty

This manipulation consists of the fact that after a short conversation, the manipulator suddenly confidentially tells the object he has chosen to manipulate that he intends to communicate something secret and important, which is intended only for him because he liked this person. He feels that he can trust him with the truth. At the same time, the object of manipulation unconsciously arises confidence in this kind of revelation, which means that we can already talk about the weakening of the protective mechanisms of the psyche, which, through the weakening of censorship (criticality barrier), passes the lies of the manipulator into the subconscious mind.

Protection - do not succumb to provocations, and remember that you can always rely only on yourself. Another person can always fail (consciously, unconsciously, under duress, under the influence of hypnosis, etc.)

29. A sudden counterargument, or insidious lie

The manipulator, unexpectedly for the object of manipulation, refers to words supposedly spoken earlier, according to which the manipulator simply develops the theme further, starting from them. After such "revelations," the object of manipulation has a feeling of guilt. The barriers put forward in the way of those words of the manipulator that he previously perceived with a certain degree of criticality should finally break down in his psyche. This is also possible because the majority of those targeted by manipulation are internally unstable, have increased criticality about themselves, and therefore, such a lie on the part of the manipulator turns, in their consciousness, into one or another piece of truth, which, as a result, helps the manipulator to get things done.

Protection - the development of willpower, exceptional confidence and self-respect.

30. The accusation of theory, or imaginary lack of practice

As an unexpected counterargument, the manipulator puts forward a demand according to which the words of the object of manipulation chosen by him are kind of good only in theory, while in practice, the situation will supposedly be different. Thus, unconsciously making it clear to the object of manipulation that all the words just heard by the manipulator are nothing and are good only on paper, but in the real situation, everything will turn out differently, which means that you cannot rely on such words.

Protection - do not pay attention to the speculations and assumptions of other people and believe only in your mind's power.

- The second block of manipulation techniques

Ways To Influence The Media Audience Through Manipulation

1. The principle of priority

This method's essence is based on the specifics of the psyche, which is structured in such a way that it takes for granted the information that was first received by the consciousness. It is also no longer necessary that we get more accurate information later.

In this case, perceiving primary information as truth is triggered, especially since it is impossible to understand its contradictory nature immediately. And after that, it is already difficult enough to change the formed opinion.

A similar principle is quite successfully used in political technologies when some accusatory material (compromising material) is sent to a competitor (through the media), thereby:

- Forming voters with a negative opinion about

him.

- Forcing to make excuses.

(In this case, there is an impact on the masses through widespread stereotypes that if someone makes excuses, it means to blame).

2. "Witnesses" of events

Ostensibly there are eyewitnesses of events who, with the necessary sincerity, report information transmitted in advance by manipulators, passing it off as their own. The name of such "eyewitnesses" is often hidden ostensibly for the conspiracy, or a false name is called, which, along with falsified information, nevertheless achieves an effect in the audience, since it affects the unconscious psyche of a person, causing the intensity of feelings and emotions in him. As a result, the censorship of the mind is weakened and can pass information from the manipulator without identifying its false essence.

3. The image of the enemy

By artificially creating a threat and, as a result of this, passions, the masses are plunged into states similar to ASC (altered states of consciousness). As a result, such weights are easier to control.

4. The shift in emphasis

In this case, a deliberate shift in emphasis occurs in the material presented, and something not quite desirable for the manipulators is shown in the background, but the opposite is highlighted — what they need.

5. Use of "opinion leaders"

In this case, the manipulations of the mass consciousness proceed on the basis that when specific actions are taken, individuals are guided by opinion leaders. Various figures may become leaders of opinions that have become authoritative in a particular category of the population.

6. Reorienting attention

In this case, almost any material can be generated without fear of its unwanted (dangerous) portion. This becomes possible based on the rule of reorienting attention when the information necessary for hiding seems to recede into the shadow of seemingly randomly displayed events that serve to distract attention.

7. Emotional charging

This technology of manipulation is based on such a property of the human psyche as emotional infectivity. In the process of life, a person builds specific protective barriers to obtaining undesirable information for him. To circumvent such a restriction (censorship of the psyche), the manipulative effect must be directed to the senses. Thus, by "charging" the necessary information with the underlying emotions, the obstacle to the mind can be surmounted. A person's emotions will erupt, forcing him to worry at some point about the information he has heard. Then comes the effect of emotional charge, which is most prevalent in the crowd, where, as you know, the criticality threshold is lower.

(Example. A similar effect of manipulation is used during a

series of reality shows when participants speak in elevated tones and sometimes show significant emotional excitement, which makes them watch the events they demonstrate and empathize with the main characters. Or, for example, when speaking on television, especially ambitious politicians who impulsively shout out their ways out of crises, due to which information affects the feelings of individuals, and emotional contagion occurs in the audience, which means that the ability of such manipulators to force attention to the material presented is increased.)

8. The ostentatious issues

Depending on the presentation of the same materials, different, sometimes opposing, opinions can be obtained from the audience. That is, some event can be artificially "not noticed," but on the contrary, be paid increased attention, and even on different television channels. At the same time, truth itself seems to fade into the background. And it depends on the desire (or lack of desire) of the manipulators to highlight it. (For example, it is known that many events take place in the country every day. Naturally, coverage of all of them is physical impossible. However, it often happens that some events are shown often, frequently, and on various channels, while something else, which probably also deserves attention is as if deliberately not seen.)

It is worth noting that the flow of information through such a manipulative technique leads to the artificial inflation of non-existent problems. Something important is not noticed that can cause the anger of the people.

9. Inaccessibility of information

This principle of manipulative technologies is called information blockade. This becomes possible when a particular piece of information, undesirable for manipulators, is deliberately not allowed.

10. Strike ahead of the curve

A type of manipulation based on the early release of negative information for the main category of people. Moreover, this information causes maximum resonance. And by the time of the subsequent receipt of information and the need for an unpopular decision, the audience will already be tired of the protest and will not react too negatively. Using a similar method in political technologies, they first sacrifice some incriminating evidence. Then, when new incriminating evidence appears on the politician they are promoting, the masses no longer react. (Tired of responding.)

11. Dishonorable passions

A way of manipulating the mass media audience when using false passions by presenting allegedly sensational material, as a result of which the human psyche does not have time to react appropriately, creates unnecessary excitement, and the information presented later does not have such an effect, because the criticality decreases due to the censorship of the psyche. (In other words, a false time limit is created for which the information received must be estimated, which often leads to the fact that it almost without cuts from the side of consciousness falls into the unconscious individual; after which it affects the knowledge, distorting the very meaning of the information received, and also taking the place to gain and appraise the information more truthful.

12. The likelihood effect

In this case, the basis for possible manipulation consists of such a component of the psyche when a person is inclined to believe information that does not contradict his previously available information or ideas on the subject under discussion.

(In other words, if through the media we come across information that we do not internally agree with, then we consciously block such a channel for obtaining information. And if we encounter information that does not contradict our understanding of such a question, we continue to absorb such information that reinforces the earlier shaped patterns of behavior, and the installation in the subconscious mind. Also, by a similar principle of manipulation, it is possible to initially supply information that is unfavorable for the manipulator (supposedly criticizing himself), thereby increasing the audience's confidence that this mass media source is relatively honest and truthful. Well, later on, the information necessary for the manipulators is interspersed in the supplied information.)

13. The effect of "information assault"

In this case, it should be said that a flurry of useless

information collapses on a person, in which truth is lost.

(People who have undergone this form of manipulation just get tired of the flow of information, which means that analyzing such information becomes difficult and manipulators can hide the information they need, but undesirable for a demonstration to the masses.)

14. The opposite effect

In the case of such a fact of manipulation, such an amount of negative information is released to some person that this information achieves the exact opposite effect. Instead of the expected conviction, such a person begins to cause pity. (An example of the Perestroika years with B.N. Yeltsin, who fell into the river from a bridge.)

15. The everyday story, or evil with a human face

Information that may cause an undesirable effect is pronounced in the usual tone as if nothing terrible was happening. This way of delivering knowledge loses its importance when it comes to audience consciousness—any important facts. Thus, the criticality of the human psyche of negative information disappears, and addiction to it occurs.

16. One-sided coverage of events

This manipulation method is aimed at one-sided coverage of events, when it is possible to speak only on one side of the process, as a result of which a false semantic effect of the information obtained is achieved.

17. The principle of contrast

This manipulation becomes possible when the necessary information is presented against the background of another, initially harmful, and negatively perceived by the majority of the audience. (In other words, against the black background, there will always be noticeable white. And against the backdrop of bad people, you can still show the right person by talking about his good deeds. A similar principle is universal in political technologies when, at first, a possible crisis in the rival camp is examined in detail. Then the true nature of the actions needed by the manipulators of a candidate who does not and cannot have such a crisis is demonstrated.)

18. Endorsement of the imaginary majority

The application of this mass manipulation technique is based on such a specific component of the human psyche as the permissibility of performing any action, after the initial approval by other people. As a result of this manipulation method in the human mind, the criticality barrier is erased after other people have approved such information. Let us recall Lebon, Freud, Ankylosing spondylitis, and other classics of the masses' psychology — the principles of imitation and infectivity are actively operating among the masses. Therefore, what one does — pick up the rest.

19. Emotional punch

When implemented, this principle should produce the effect of psychological shock, when manipulators achieve the desired result by intentionally broadcasting the horrors of modern life, which causes the first reaction of protest (because of the fast development of the psyche emotion), and the desire to punish the guilty at all costs. At the same time, they do not notice that the emphasis in the presentation of the material can be deliberately shifted towards competitors that are unnecessary for manipulators or against information that seems undesirable.

20. False analogies, or sabotage against logic

This manipulation removes the exact cause in a question, replacing it with a false analogy. (For example, there is an incorrect comparison of various and mutually exclusive consequences, which in this case are presented as one. For example, many young athletes were selected in the State Duma of the last convocation. In this case, the merits in sports in the minds of the masses replaced the opinion that the 20-year-olds athletes can rule the country, but remember that every State Duma deputy has the rank of federal minister).

21. Artificial "miscalculation" of the situation

A lot of different information is deliberately thrown onto the market, thereby tracking public interest in this information, and knowledge that has not gained relevance is subsequently excluded.

22. Manipulative commenting

Through the accent necessary for the manipulators, an event is highlighted. In this case, any event undesirable for manipulators when using such technology can take the opposite color. It all depends on how the manipulators present this or that material, with which comments.

23. The effect of presence

The link to the presence at any event allows you to direct the manipulative technique to the maximum achievement of the desired result. By type — an eyewitness is always right.

24. Admission (approximation) to power

This manipulation is based on such a property of the psyche of most individuals as a radical change in their views if such a person is endowed with the necessary authority. (A rather striking example is D.O. Rogozin, who was in opposition to the authorities. We recall the statement of Rogozin in connection with the ban of the CEC on the registration of V. Gerashchenko as a presidential candidate. We remember the hunger strike in the State Duma with the demands for the resignation of the ministers of the socio-economic block of the government. We recall other statements by Rogozin, including about the party in power and the president of the country, and remember Rogozin's speeches after he is appointed permanent representative of Russia to the North Atlantic Treaty Organization (NATO) in Brussels, i.e., nickname representing Russia in an enemy organization.)

25. Repetition

A similar method of manipulation is quite simple. It is only necessary to repeatedly give any information so that such information is deposited in the mass media audience's memory and is subsequently used. Simultaneously, manipulators should simplify the text as much as possible and achieve its susceptibility in the calculation of a low-intellectual public. Oddly enough, practically only in this case you can be sure that the necessary information will not only be conveyed to the mass viewer, reader, or listener but also will be correctly perceived by them. And this effect can be achieved by consistent repetition of simple phrases. In this case, the information is first firmly entrenched in the subconscious mind of the listeners. Then it will affect their consciousness, and therefore the performance of actions, the semantic connotation of which is secretly laid down in the information for the mass media audience.

26. The truth is half

In this method of manipulation, only part of the reliable information is presented to the public. In contrast, the other section, explaining the possibility of the existence of the first part, is hidden by the manipulators. (An example of the times of Perestroika, when rumors were first circulated that the Union republics allegedly contained the RSFSR. At the same time, they forgot about Russian subsidies. As a result of deceiving the republics' population that are friendly to us, these republics first left the USSR. Afterward, part of their community began to come to earnings to Russia.)

- The third block of manipulation techniques

Speech Psychotechnics

In the event of such an impact, it is forbidden to use direct information impact methods, spoken in an orderly manner, replacing the latter with a request or proposal, and at the same time using the following verbal tricks:

1) Truisms

In this case, the manipulator pronounces what is in reality, but in fact, in his words, a fraudulent strategy is hidden. For example, a manipulator wants to sell goods in a beautiful package in a deserted place. He does not say: "buy"! Instead he says: "Well, the cold! These are great, very cheap sweaters! Everyone buys, you won't find such cheap sweaters anywhere!" and twirls packets of sweaters in his hands.

As noted by Academician V.M. Kandyba, such an unobtrusive purchase offer, is more focused on the subconscious, works better, as it corresponds to the truth and passes the critical barrier of consciousness. It is really "cold" (this is one unconscious "yes"), indeed the package and pattern of the sweater are beautiful (the second "yes"), and really very cheap (the third "yes"). Therefore, without any use of the word, "Buy!" it seems to him that an object of manipulation is born an independent decision made by him to buy at a cheap price and on the occasion an excellent thing, often without even unrolling the package, but only asking for the size.

2) The illusion of choice

In this case, as if in a usual phrase of the manipulator about the presence of any product or phenomenon, some hidden statement is interspersed, which flawlessly acts on the subconscious, forcing to fulfill the will of the manipulator. For example, they do not ask you whether you will buy or not, but say: "How pretty you are! This suits you, and it looks great! Which one will you take, this or this?" and the manipulator looks at you with sympathy, as if the question that you are buying this thing has already been resolved. Indeed, the last phrase of the manipulator contains a trap for consciousness that imitates your right to choose. But in fact, you are being deceived, since the choice "buy - do not buy" has been replaced by the choice "buy this or buy that."

3) Teams hidden in questions

In this case, the manipulator hides his installation command under the guise of a request. For example, you need to close the door. You can say to someone: "Go and close the door!" But it will be worse than if your order was issued with a request in the question: "Could you kindly close the door?" The second option works better, and the person does not feel cheated.

4) The moral impasse

This case is a hoax of consciousness; the manipulator, asking for an opinion on a product, after receiving an answer, asks the next question, which contains the statement on the execution of the action required by the manipulator. For example, the seller-manipulator persuades not to buy, but "just try" his goods. In this case, we have a trap for consciousness, since it seems that nothing dangerous or bad is offered to him and it seems that complete freedom of any decision is preserved, but in fact it's enough to try, as the seller asks another tricky question right away: "Well, did you like it? Did you like it?" And although it seems to be about tastes, but in fact the question is: "Will you buy or not?" And since the thing is objectively tasty, you can't say to the seller's question that you didn't like it, and answer that you "liked", thereby giving involuntary consent to the purchase. Moreover, as soon as you answer the seller that you liked it, he, without waiting for your other words, already weighs the goods and it's as if it's inconvenient for you to refuse the purchase, especially since the seller selects and imposes the best that he has (from that which is visible). Conclusion - you need to think a hundred times before accepting a seemingly innocuous offer.

5) Speech reception: "than ... - so ..."

The essence of this speech psychotechnology is that the manipulator connects what is happening with what he needs. For example, the seller of hats, seeing that the buyer turns the hat in his hands for a long time, deciding to buy or not to buy, says that the customer is lucky, because he found exactly the hat that suits him best. Like, "The more I look at you, the more I am convinced that this is so."

6) Coding

After the manipulation has worked, the manipulators encode their victim into amnesia (forgetting) of everything that happens. For example, if a gypsy (as an extra-class specialist in waking hypnosis, street manipulation) took the ring or chain from the victim, then she will definitely say the phrase: "You do not know me and you have never seen them! These things — the ring and the chain — are strangers! You have never seen them!" In this case, if the

115

hypnosis was not deep, the charm ("charm" - as an essential part of waking suggestion) disappears in a few minutes. With deep hypnosis, coding can persist for years.

7) The Stirlitz method

Since a person in any conversation better remembers the beginning and the end, it is necessary not only to enter the conversation correctly, but also that the necessary words that the manipulation object must remember are put at the end of the conversation.

8) The speech trick "three stories"

In the case of such a technique, the next method of programming the human psyche is carried out. You are told some three stories. But in an unusual way. First, they begin to tell you story No. 1. In the middle, they interrupt it and begin to tell story No. 2. In the middle they interrupt it, and they begin to tell story No. 3, which they tell completely. Then the manipulator completes story No. 2, and then completes story No. 1. As a result of this method of programming the psyche, history No. 1 and No. 2 are recognized and remembered. And story No. 3 is quickly forgotten and unrecognized, which means that, being squeezed out of consciousness, it is placed in the subconscious. But the bottom line is that manipulators laid instructions and commands for the subconscious of the manipulation object in the story No. 3, which means you can be sure that after a while this person (manipulation object) will begin to fulfill the psychological settings introduced into his subconscious, and at the same time he will assume that they come from him. The introduction of information into the subconscious is a reliable way of programming a person to perform the settings necessary for manipulators.

9) Allegory

As a result of such an impact of the processing of consciousness, the information needed by the manipulator is hidden among the history, which the manipulator sets out allegorically and metaphorically. The bottom line is that just the hidden meaning is the thought that the manipulator decided to put into your consciousness. Moreover, the brighter and more picturesque the story is told, the easier it is for such information to go around the criticality barrier and introduce information into the subconscious. Later, such information "begins to work" often just at the moment, the onset of which was originally laid down; or a code was laid down, activated by the manipulator each time to achieve the necessary effect.

10) The method "as soon as ... then ..."

Very interesting method. This speech technique-trick is one that a gypsy, for example, foreseeing some likely future action of a client, says, for example: "As soon as you see your line life, immediately understand me!" Here, by the subconscious logic of the client's view of her palm (the "lifeline"), the gypsy logically connects building confidence in herself and everything that she does. At the same time, the gypsy cleverly inserts a trap for consciousness at the end of the phrase "immediately understand me", the intonation of which means a different meaning, hidden from consciousness, "immediately agree with everything that I do."

11) Dispersion

The method is quite interesting and effective. It consists in the fact that the manipulator, telling you a story, selects its settings in some way that violates the monotony of speech, including the so-called "anchors" (the "anchoring" technique refers to neurolinguistic programming techniques). It is possible to distinguish speech by intonation, volume, touch, gestures, etc. Thus, such attitudes seem to be scattered among the other words that make up the information flow of a given story. And later, the subconscious of the object of manipulation will only respond to these words, intonations, gestures and so on. In addition, as Academician V.M. Kandyba notes, hidden teams scattered among the entire conversation turn out to be very effective and work much better than those expressed otherwise.

The following methods of manipulative influences on the subconscious are distinguished in order to program human behavior (object of manipulation):

- Kinesthetic methods (the most effective): touching the hand, touching the head, any stroking, patting on the shoulder, shaking hands, touching the fingers, applying brushes on the client's hands from above, taking the client's brush in both hands, etc.
- Emotional ways: raising emotions at the right time,

lowering emotions, emotional exclamations or gestures.

- Speech methods: change the volume of speech (louder, quieter); change in the pace of speech (faster, slower, pause); change in intonation (increase-decrease); related sounds (tapping, snapping fingers); change the localization of the sound source (right, left, top, bottom, front, back); change in the tone of voice (imperative, command, hard, soft, insinuating, lingering).

- Visual methods: facial expressions, eye expansion, hand gestures, finger movements, changing body position (tilting, turning), changing the position of the head (turning, tilting, lifting), a characteristic sequence of gestures (pantomime), rubbing your own chin.

- Written ways. In any written text, using the dispersion technique, you can insert hidden information, while the necessary words are distinguished: font size, different font, different color, indentation, new line, etc.

12) The "old reaction" method

According to this method, it is necessary to remember that if in a situation a person reacts strongly to a stimulus, then after a while you can expose that person to the action of such a stimulus, and the old reaction will automatically work, although the conditions and situation may vary significantly from the one in which the reaction manifested itself for the first time. A classic example of an "old reaction" is when a dog suddenly attacks a child walking in a park. The child was very frightened and subsequently in any situation, even with the safest and most harmless, when he sees a dog, automatically and unconsciously, the "old reaction" arises: fear.

Such reactions can result from pain, temperature, kinesthetic (touch), taste, auditory, olfactory, etc., therefore, according to the mechanism of the "old reaction" it is necessary to fulfill a number of basic conditions:

I.   The reflexive reaction should be fixed as many times as possible.
II.   The applied stimulus should in its characteristics match the irritant used for the first time.
III. The best and most reliable is a complex stimulus that uses the reaction of several senses simultaneously.

If you need to establish the dependence of another person on you (the object of manipulation), you must:

- Cause in the process of questioning the object a reaction of joy.
- Fix a similar reaction by any of the signaling methods (the so-called "anchors" in NLP).
- If necessary, encode the psyche of the object - "activate" the "anchor" at the right time. In this case, in response to your information, which, in your opinion, should be deposited in the memory of the object, the person selected for the role of the object will have a positive associative series, which

means that the criticality barrier of the psyche will be broken, and such a person (object) will be "programmed" for implementation, conceived by you after the encoding you entered. It is recommended to check yourself several times before fixing the "anchor", so that by facial expressions, gestures, changed intonation, etc. remember the reflex reaction of the object to words positive for its psyche (for example, pleasant memories of the object), and pick up a reliable key (tilting the head, voice, touch, etc.).

- The fourth block of manipulations

Manipulation Through Television

1) Fabrication of facts

In this case, manipulation occurs as a result of small deviations used in the supply of material but always acting in the same direction. Manipulators tell the truth only when the truth can be easily verified. In other cases, they try to present the material in the way they need it. Moreover, a lie becomes most effective when it is based on a stereotype embedded in the subconscious.

2) Selection for reality events material

In this case, an effective condition for programming thinking is the control of the media to supply unified information, but in different words. At the same time, the activities of opposition media are allowed. But their activities should be controlled and not go beyond the scope of broadcasting that they allow. Also, the media use the so-called principle of democracy of noise, when a message unnecessary by a manipulator, has to die under a powerful surge of versatile information.

3) Gray and black information

In the second half of the 20th century, the media began to use psychological warfare technology. The American Military Dictionary of 1948 gives the following definition to psychological warfare: "These are systematic propaganda events that influence the views, emotions, attitudes, and behavior of the enemy, neutral or friendly foreign groups to support national politics." The manual (1964) states that the purpose of such a war is "to undermine the country's political and social structure ... to such a degree of degradation of national consciousness that the state becomes incapable of resistance."

4) Big psychoses

The secret tasks of the media are to turn the citizens of a country into a single mass (crowd), with the goal of the general regulation of the distribution of the flow of information, which processes the consciousness and subconscious of people. As a result, such a crowd is easier to manage, and the average layman unquestioningly believes the ridiculous statements.

5) Approval and repetition

In this case, the information is supplied in the form of ready-made templates that actively use the stereotypes available in the subconscious. Affirmation in any speech means refusal to discuss, because the power of the idea, which can be discussed, loses all credibility. In human thinking, notes Kara-Murza, is the so-called mosaic type of culture. Media are a factor in strengthening this type of thinking, teaching a person to think in stereotypes, and not include intelligence when analyzing media materials. G. Lebon noted that with the help of repetition, information is introduced into the subconscious' depths, where motives of subsequent actions of a person arise. Excessive repetition dulls the mind, causing any information to be deposited in the subconscious mind with virtually no change.

6) Crushing and urgency

In this technique of manipulating the media used, integral information is divided into fragments, so that a person could not combine them into a single whole and comprehend the problem. (For example, articles in a newspaper are divided into parts and placed on different pages; text or a telecast is broken by advertising.) Professor G. Schiller explains the effectiveness of this technique: "When the integral nature of a social problem is intentionally bypassed, and fragmentary information about it is offered as reliable "Information," the results of this approach are always the same: misunderstanding...apathy and, as a rule, indifference." Tearing pieces of information about an important event, it is possible to drastically reduce the impact of the message or completely deprive it of meaning.

7) Simplification, stereotyping

This type of manipulation is based on the fact that a person is a product of a mosaic culture. The media create his mind. Media, in contrast to high culture, is designed specifically for the masses. Therefore, they imposed strict restrictions on the complexity and originality of messages. The justification for this is the rule that the representative of the mass can adequately absorb only simple information, so any new information is adapted to the stereotype so that a person perceives information without effort and internal analysis.

8) Sensationalism

In this case, the principle of such a presentation of information is retained when it is impossible or very difficult to form a single whole from separate parts. In this case, any pseudo-sensation is highlighted. And already under cover of it, the really important news is hushed up (if this news is dangerous for some reason to the circles that control the media).

The continuous bombardment of consciousness, especially by the "bad news," performs an important function of maintaining the necessary level of "nervousness" in society, according to prof. S.G. Kara-Murza. Such nervousness, a feeling of continuous crisis, dramatically increases the suggestibility of people and reduces the ability to critical perception.

9) Change the meaning of words and concepts

Manipulators from the media, in this case, freely interpret

the words of any person. In this case, the context changes, often taking the form directly opposite or at least distorted. Prof S.G. Kara-Murza gives a vivid example, telling that when the Pope during a visit to one of the countries was asked how he relates to houses of tolerance, was surprised that they supposedly exist. After that, an emergency message appeared in the newspapers: "The first thing my dad asked when he stepped on our land was, 'Is there tolerance at home?'"

- The fifth block of manipulations

Manipulations Of Consciousness

1. Provocation of suspicion

The manipulator initially puts the subject in critical condition when he confidently puts forward a statement like: "Do you think I will persuade you?" suggesting the implied. The opposite effect, when the one over whom the manipulations are carried out, begins to convince the manipulator of the opposite, and thereby, saying the installation several times, unconsciously inclines to the opinion of honesty in something convincing him. Whereas under all conditions, this honesty is false. But under certain conditions, he would understand that the line between the lie and the receptivity of truth is erased in this situation. So the manipulator is achieving his goal.

Protection - do not pay attention, believe in yourself.

2. False advantage of the enemy

The manipulator, in his own specific words, as if initially, casts doubt on his arguments, referring to the supposedly more favorable conditions in which his opponent is. This, in turn, makes this opponent make excuses for wanting to convince a partner and remove suspicion. Thus, the one over whom the manipulation took place unconsciously relieves himself of any attitude towards censorship of the psyche, to defense, allowing him to penetrate his defenseless psyche attacks from the manipulator. The words of the manipulator, possible in a similar situation: "You say so because now your position requires it ..."

Protection - such words as: "Yes, I say that because I have such a position, I'm right, and you must obey me."

3. Aggressive conversation

Using this technique, the manipulator takes an initially high and aggressive pace of speech, which unconsciously denies the opponent's will. Also, the opponent, in this case, cannot properly process all the information received. What forces him to agree with the information from the manipulator, unconsciously also wanting to stop all this as soon as possible.

Protection - make an artificial pause, interrupt the fast pace, reduce the aggressive intensity of the conversation, and dialogue in a calm direction. If necessary, you can retire for a while, i.e., interrupt the conversation and then — when the manipulator calms down — continue the conversation.

4. Imaginary misunderstanding

In this case, a certain trick is achieved as follows. The manipulator, referring to clarifying the correctness of what you just heard, repeats the words you said, but making your sense in them. Spoken words can be like: "Sorry, if I understand you correctly, you say that ..." and then he repeats 60-70% of what he heard from you, but distorts the final meaning by entering other information — information necessary for him.

Protection - a clear clarification, returning and re-explaining to the manipulator what you had in mind when you said, so-and-so.

5. False agreement

In this case, the manipulator seems to agree with the information received from you but immediately makes his adjustments. According to the principle: "Yes, yes, everything is correct, but ...".

Protection - believe in yourself and do not pay attention to manipulative techniques in a conversation with you.

6. Provocation to scandal

In time with the said offensive words, the manipulator tries to provoke anger, rage, misunderstanding, resentment, etc., with his ridicule to get you crazy and achieve the intended result.

Protection is a firm character, a strong will, a cold mind.

7. Specific terminology

In this way, the manipulator makes you unconsciously lower your status, as well as develop a feeling of inconvenience, as a result of which you are embarrassed to ask the meaning of a term out of false modesty or self-doubt, which allows the manipulator to turn the situation into the right direction, citing the need for your alleged approval of the words he said earlier. Lowering the interlocutor's status in the conversation allows you to find yourself in an initially winning position and eventually achieve the necessary.

Protection - ask again, clarify, pause, and go back if necessary, referring to the desire to understand better what is required of you.

8. Using the effect of false suspicion in your words

Applying a similar position of psycho-influence, the manipulator, as it were, initially puts the interlocutor in the position of the defender. An example of the monologue used: "Do you think I will convince you of something...", which, as it were, makes the object want to convince the manipulator that it's not so, that you are well located to it (to the manipulator), etc. Thus, as it were, the subject reveals himself for unconscious agreement with the words of the manipulator that follow after this.

Protection - words such as: "Yes. I think that you should try to convince me of this. Otherwise, I won't believe you, and further conversation will not work. "

9. Reference to the "greats"

The manipulator operates with quotes from the speeches of famous and significant people, the specifics of the principles adopted in society, and so on. Thus, the manipulator unknowingly lowers your status. They say; look, all respected and well-known people say so. You think very differently, who you are, who they are, etc. Approximately the same associative chain should unconsciously appear at the object of manipulation, after which the person becomes such an object.

Protection - faith in one's exclusivity and "chosenness."

10. The formation of false stupidity and failure

Sayings like - this is corny, it is complete bad taste and so on - must form the manipulation object's initial unconscious diminution of his role and form his artificial dependence on others' opinions, which prepares the dependence of the person on the manipulator. This means that the manipulator can practically safely advance his ideas through the manipulation object, moving the object to solve the problems needed by the manipulator. In other words, the ground for manipulation has already been prepared by the manipulations themselves.

Protection - do not succumb to provocations and believe in your mind, knowledge, experience, education, etc.

11. The imposition of thoughts

In this case, through constantly or periodically repeated phrases, the manipulator accustoms the object to any information conveyed to him.

The principle of advertising is built on such manipulation. When at first, some information appears before a person (moreover, regardless of his conscious approval or denial of it), or when a person is faced with the need to choose a product, he unconsciously selects one of several types of goods of unknown brands that are already heard somewhere. Moreover, based on the fact that through advertising, an exclusively positive opinion is heard about a product, it is much more likely that an exclusively positive opinion about this product is formed in an unconscious person.

Protection - the initial critical analysis of any information received.

12. Proof, with hints of some special circumstances

This is a way of manipulation through a special kind of an understatement, which forms false confidence in what has been said in the object of manipulation using the unconscious thought of one or another situation by it. And when in the end it turns out that he "misunderstood," such a person practically does not have any component of the protest, because unconsciously he remains sure that he is guilty. After all, he did not understand it. Thus, the object of manipulation is forced (unconsciously) to accept the rules of the game imposed on him.

In the context of such a circumstance, it most likely makes sense to divide it into manipulation, taking into account both unexpected for the object and forced, when the subject eventually realizes that he has become a victim of manipulations. But he is forced to accept them because of the impossibility of conflict with his conscience embedded into his psyche by attitudes in the form of norms of behavior based on certain principles of society that prevent such a person (object) from reversing. Moreover, the agreement on his part can be dictated by a falsely evoked sense of guilt in him, and a kind of moral masochism, which forces him to punish himself unconsciously.

13. Imaginary inattention

In this situation, the manipulation object falls into the trap of the manipulator, playing on his own supposedly inattention, so that after having achieved his own, he refers to the fact that he allegedly did not notice (listen to) the protest from the opponent. At the same time, he actually puts the object of manipulation before the fact of the perfect.

Protection - to clarify and ask again what you misunderstood.

14. The humiliation of irony

As a result of the thoughts spoken at the right time about the insignificance of one's status, the manipulator seems to force the object to assert the opposite and, in every way, elevate the manipulator. Thus, subsequent manipulative actions of the manipulator become invisible to the object of manipulation.

Protection - if the manipulator believes that it is "insignificant" - it is necessary to continue to give his will, reinforcing that feeling in him so that he no longer has thoughts to manipulate you. When you see the manipulator, there is a desire to obey you or to bypass you.

15. Focus on the pros

In this case, the manipulator concentrates the conversation only on the pluses, thereby promoting his idea and ultimately manipulating the psyche of another person.

Defense - to make several conflicting statements, to be able to say no, etc.

- Sixth block of manipulations

Manipulation Of Personality

1. "Labeling"

This technique consists of choosing offensive epithets, metaphors, names, etc. ("labels") to denote a person, organization, idea, or social phenomenon. Such "labels" cause an emotionally negative attitude of others, they associate with low (dishonest and socially disapproving) actions (behavior) and, thus, are used to discredit a person, expressed ideas and suggestions, organization, social group or subject of discussion in the eyes of the audience.

2. "Shining generalizations"

This technique consists of replacing the name or designation of a particular social phenomenon, idea, organization, social group, or specific person with a more general name that has a positive emotional connotation and causes others' friendly attitude. This technique is based on the exploitation of positive feelings and emotions of people towards certain concepts and words, for example, such as "freedom," "patriotism," "peace," "happiness," "love," "success," "victory," etc. Such words, bearing a positive psycho-emotional impact, are used to drag decisions beneficial to a particular person, group, or organization.

3. "Transfer" or "Switch"

The essence of this technique consists in skillfully, unobtrusively, and invisibly to most people, spreading the authority and prestige of what they value and respect for what the source of communication presents to them. Using the "transfer," associative relations of the presented object are formed with someone or something with value and significance, among others. A negative "transfer" is also used to create associations with negative and socially unapproved events, actions, facts, people, etc., which is necessary to discredit specific individuals, ideas, situations, social groups, or organizations.

4. "Link to authorities"

The content of this technique is to cite individuals with high authority or vice versa, which causes a negative reaction in the category of people who are being manipulated. The statements used usually contain value judgments about people, ideas, events, etc., and express their condemnation or approval. Thus, as an object of manipulative influence, a person initiates the formation of the corresponding relationship — positive or negative.

5. "The game of common people"

The purpose of this technique is to establish trusting

relationships with the audience, as with similar-minded people, that both the manipulator and the ideas are correct, as they are oriented to the common person. This technique is actively used in advertising and informational promotion and various propaganda for the formation of the chosen image — "a person from the people" — to build trust in him from the people.

6. "Shuffle" or "juggling cards"

The content of this technique consists in the selection and intentional presentation of only positive or only negative facts and arguments, while at the same time ignoring the opposite. Its main goal — using one-sided selection and presentation of facts — shows the attractiveness, or vice versa, the unacceptability of any point of view, program, or idea.

7. "General carriage"

When using this technique, judgments, statements, phrases are required that require uniformity in behavior, creating the impression that everyone does it. For example, a message can begin with the words: "All normal people understand that ..." or "No sane person will object that ...", etc. Through the "common platform," a person is convinced that the majority of members of a certain social community with whom he identifies himself or whose opinion is significant for him, accept similar values, ideas, or programs.

8. Crushing information, redundancy, high pace

Often, such tricks are used on television. As a result of such a massive shelling of people's consciousness (for example, cruelty on TV), they cease to critically perceive what is happening and perceive it as meaningless incidents. The viewer, following the quick speech of the announcer or presenter, misses links to the source of information and, in his imagination, already connects and agrees with all the inconsistent parts of the perceived programs.

9. "Mockery"

When using this technique, both specific individuals, views, ideas, programs, organizations, and their activities or various associations of people who are being fought can be ridiculed. The choice of the object of ridicule is carried out depending on the goals and the specific information and communication situation. The effect of this technique is based on the fact that when ridiculing individual statements and elements of human behavior, a humorous and frivolous attitude is initiated towards the person, which automatically applies to his other statements and views. With the skillful use of such a technique, it is possible to form the image of a "frivolous" person, whose statements are not credible, for a particular person.

10. "The method of negative reference groups"

In this case, it is argued that any set of views is the only correct one. All who share these views are better than those who do not (but share others, often opposed). For example, pioneers or Komsomol members are better than informal youth. Pioneers and Komsomol members are honest, responsive, and if Komsomol members are called up for military service, they are excellent students in military and political training. And informal youth — punks, hippies, and so on — are not good youth. Thus one group is opposed to another. Accordingly, various accents of perception are highlighted.

11. "Repeating slogans" or "repeating template phrases"

The main condition for the effective use of this technique is the correct slogan. A slogan is a short statement, formulated in such a way as to attract attention and influence the imagination and feelings of the reader or listener. The slogan should be adapted to the characteristics of the target audience (i.e., groups of people who need to be affected). Using the technique of "repeating slogans" implies that the listener or reader will not think about the meaning of individual words used in the slogan, nor about the correctness of the whole wording. We can add to the definition of G. Grachev and I. Melnik that the brevity of the slogan allows information to penetrate the subconscious freely, thereby programming the psyche, and giving rise to psychological attitudes and patterns of behavior.

12. "Emotional adjustment"

This technique can be defined as a way of creating a mood while transmitting certain information. The mood is caused by various means (external environment, a certain time of day, lighting, light stimulants, music, songs, etc.). Against this background, the relevant information is transmitted, but strives to ensure that it is not too much. This technique is often used in theatrical performances, game and show programs, religious (cult) events, etc.

13. "Promotion through mediators"

This technique is based on the fact that the process of perceiving relevant information, certain values, views, ideas, and evaluations has a two-stage nature. This means that an effective informational impact on a person is often carried out not through the media, but through people that are authoritative for him. This phenomenon is reflected in the two-stage communication flow model developed by Paul Lazarsfeld in the mid-1950s. In the model he proposed, the distinguished two-step process of the mass communication process is taken into account, firstly, as the interaction between the communicator and the "opinion leaders," and secondly, as the interaction of opinion leaders with members of micro-social groups. "Leaders of opinions" may include informal leaders, political figures, representatives of religious faiths, cultural, scientific, and artistic figures, athletes, military, etc. In the practice of the informational and psychological impact of the media, this has led to the fact that outreach and advertising messages have become more focused on people whose opinions are significant for others. (i.e., ratings and advertising promotion of goods are carried out by "movie stars" and other popular persons). The manipulative effect is enhanced by interspersing with entertainment programs, interviews, direct or indirect assessments of such leaders of any ongoing events, and contributing to the desired impact on the subconscious level of the human psyche.

14. "Imaginary choice"

The essence of this technique lies in the fact that listeners or readers are informed of several different points of view on a particular issue, but in such a way that they gradually present in the most favorable light the one that they want to be accepted by the audience. For this, several additional tricks are usually used:

a) Include in the propaganda materials the so-called "two-way messages," which contain arguments for and against a certain position. The opponent's arguments preempt, such as "two-way communication".

b) Positive and negative elements are dosed. For a positive assessment to look more plausible, a little criticism needs to be added to the characterization of the described point of view, and the effectiveness of a condemning position increases if there are elements of praise.

c) Selection of facts of strengthening or weakening of statements is carried out. Conclusions are not included in the text of the above messages. They should be made by those for whom the information is intended.

d) There is an operation with comparative materials to enhance the importance, demonstrate the trends and scale of events, and phenomena. In this case, all the actual data used are selected so that the necessary conclusion is sufficiently obvious.

15. "Initiation of the information wave"

An effective technique of informational impact on large groups of people is the initiation of a secondary informational wave. An event is proposed that will pick up and begin to circulate the media. At the same time, other media can pick up the initial coverage in one media, which will increase the power of information and psychological impact. This creates the so-called "Primary" informational wave. The main purpose of this technique is to create a secondary information wave at the level of interpersonal communication by initiating relevant discussions, assessments, and rumors. All this allows you to enhance the effect of the information-psychological impact on target audiences.

- Seventh block of manipulations

Manipulative Techniques Used In The Course Of Discussions And Interactions

1. Dosing of the initial information base

Materials needed for discussion are not provided to participants on time or are given selectively. An "incomplete set of materials" is handed out to some participants in the discussions, "as if by accident." Over time, it turns out that someone, unfortunately, was not aware of all the available information — working documents, letters, appeals, notes, and everything else that is "lost" that can affect the process, and the discussion results are disadvantageous. Thus, incomplete informing of some participants is carried out, which makes discussion difficult for them, and for others creates additional opportunities for the use of psychological manipulations.

2. " Excessive information"

Reverse option. It consists in the fact that too many projects, proposals, solutions, etc. are being prepared, the comparison of which in the discussion process is impossible. Especially when a large amount of materials are proposed for discussion in a short time, their qualitative analysis is difficult.

3. Formation of opinions through a targeted selection of speakers

The word is given first to those whose opinion is known and suits the organizer of manipulative influence. In this way, the formation of the desired setting is carried out among the participants in the discussion because changing the primary setting requires more effort than its formation. To carry out the formation of the settings necessary for the manipulators, the discussion can also end or be interrupted after the speech of a person whose position corresponds to the manipulators' views.

4. A double standard in the norms of assessing the behavior of participants in discussions

Some speakers are severely limited in compliance with the rules of relations during the discussion; others are allowed to move away from them and violate established rules. The same thing happens about the nature of the statements made: some do not notice harsh statements addressed to opponents, others make comments, etc. A variant is possible when the regulation is not specifically set so that you can choose a more convenient line of behavior along the way. In this case, either smoothing the positions of opponents and "pulling" them to the desired point of view is carried out. Conversely, the differences in their positions are strengthened up to incompatible and mutually exclusive points of view, as well as bringing the discussion to absurdity.

5. "Maneuvering" the list of the discussion

To make the "necessary" question easier to pass, first, "steam is let out" (initiate a surge of emotions) on insignificant questions. When everyone is tired or impressed by the previous battle, a question is raised that they want to discuss without intensified criticism.

6. Management of the discussion process

In public discussions, the word is alternately given to the most aggressive representatives of opposition groups that allow mutual insults, which are either not suppressed or suppressed only for appearance. As a result of such a manipulative move, the atmosphere of discussion is heating up to critical. Thus, a discussion of a relevant topic can be stopped. Another way is to unexpectedly interrupt an unwanted speaker, or deliberately move on to another topic. This technique is often used during commercial negotiations, when, according to a pre-agreed signal from the manager, the secretary makes coffee, an "important" call is organized, etc.

7. Limitations in the discussion procedure

When using this technique, suggestions regarding the

discussion procedure are ignored; unwanted facts, questions, arguments are circumvented; no word is given to participants who, through their statements, can lead to undesirable changes in the discussion. The decisions made are fixed rigidly, it is not allowed to return to them even when new data are received that are important for the development of final decisions.

8. Referencing

There is a brief reformulation of questions, proposals, and arguments, during which there is a shift in emphasis in the desired direction. At the same time, an arbitrary summary can be carried out. In the process of summing up the results, the emphasis in the conclusions, the presentation of the opponents' positions, their views, and the results of the discussion in the desired direction are changed. Also, with interpersonal communication, you can improve your status with the help of a certain furniture arrangement and resort to several techniques. For example, to have a visitor in a lower armchair, to have a lot of master's diplomas in his office on the walls, and in discussions and negotiations, he will demonstratively use the attributes of power and authority.

9. Psychological tricks

This group includes techniques based on the irritation of the opponent, the use of feelings of shame, carelessness, the humiliation of personal qualities, flattery, playing on self-esteem, and other individual psychological characteristics of a person.

10. The annoyance of the opponent

They are unbalancing with ridicule, unfair accusations, and other means until he "boils." It is important that the opponent becomes irritated and makes a statement that is erroneous or disadvantageous for his position in the discussion. This technique is actively used in the explicit form as a belittling of the opponent or a more veiled, in combination with irony, indirect allusions, implicit, but recognizable subtext. Acting similarly, the manipulator can emphasize, for example, such negative personality traits of the object of manipulative influence as ignorance, ignorance in a certain area, etc.

11. Self-praise

This trick is an indirect method of belittling an opponent. It's just not explicitly saying "who you are," but according to "who I am" and "who you are arguing with," the corresponding conclusion follows. Such expressions can be used: "... I am the head of a large enterprise, region, industry, institution, etc.", "... I had to solve large problems..." "...before applying for it... you need to be a leader at least ... "... before discussing and criticizing... you need to gain experience in solving problems at least on a scale ... ", etc.

12. Use of unfamiliar words, theories, and terms for the opponent

The trick succeeds if the opponent hesitates to ask again and pretends that he took these arguments, understood the meaning of terms that are unclear to him. Behind such words or phrases is the desire to discredit the personal qualities of the object of manipulation. Particularly effective from the use of unfamiliar to most slangs occurs in situations where the object of manipulation does not have the opportunity to object or clarify what was meant and can also be aggravated by the use of a fast pace of speech and a lot of thoughts that change one another during the discussion. Moreover, it is important to note that the use of scientific terms is considered manipulation only when such a statement is made consciously for the psychological impact on the object of manipulation.

13. " Lubrication" of the arguments

In this case, the manipulators play on flattery, vanity, arrogance, the increased conceit of the object of manipulation. For example, he is bribed with the words that he "... as a person of insight and erudition, intellectually developed and competent sees the internal logic of the development of this phenomenon ..." Thus, an ambitious person is faced with a dilemma — either to accept this point of view or reject a flattering public assessment and enter into a dispute, the outcome of which is not sufficiently predicted.

14. Failure or withdrawal from the discussion

A similar manipulative action is carried out with a demonstrative use of resentment. For example, "... it is impossible to discuss serious issues with you constructively..." or "... your behavior makes it impossible to continue our meeting ...", or "I am ready to continue this discussion, but only after you have calmed down... "etc.

Disruption of the discussion with the use of provoking a conflict is carried out by using various techniques to get the opponent out of himself when the discussion turns into ordinary bickering completely unrelated to the original topic. Also, tricks such as interruption, raising the voice, demonstrative acts of behavior, unwillingness to listen, and disrespect for the opponent, can be used. After their application, statements are made according to the type: "... it's impossible to talk with you because you do not give a single intelligible answer to any question "; "... it's impossible to talk with you because you are not allowing expressing a point of view that does not coincide with yours..." etc.

15. Reception "stick arguments"

They are used in two main varieties that differ in purpose. Suppose the goal is to interrupt the discussion, psychologically suppressing the opponent, a reference to the so-called higher interests without deciphering these higher interests and without arguing the reasons why they are appealed to. In this case, they use statements like: "Do you understand what you are trying to encroach on?! ...", etc. If it is necessary to force the object of manipulation to at least outwardly agree with the proposed point of view, then such arguments are used that the object can accept for fear of something unpleasant, dangerous, or to which it cannot respond by its views for the same reasons. Such arguments may include such judgments as: "... this is a denial of the constitutionally fixed institution of the presidency, the system of higher legislative bodies, undermining the constitutional foundations of society ... ".

It can simultaneously be combined with an indirect form of labeling: "... it is precisely such statements that contribute to provoking social conflicts ..." or "... Nazi leaders used such arguments in their vocabulary ...", or "... you knowingly use the facts that contribute to inciting nationalism, anti-Semitism ... ", etc.

16. "Reading in the hearts"

It is used in two main versions (the so-called positive and negative forms). The essence of using this technique is that the audience's attention shifts from the content of the opponent's arguments to the alleged reasons and hidden motives why he speaks and defends a certain point of view, and does not agree with the arguments of the opposite side. May be enhanced by the simultaneous use of "stick arguments" and "tagging." For example: "... you say that protecting corporate interests ...", or "... the reason for your aggressive criticism and irreconcilable position is obvious — this is the desire to discredit progressive forces, constructive opposition, disrupt the process of democratization ... but people will not allow such pseudo-defenders of the law to impede the satisfaction of its legitimate interests ... " etc. Sometimes "reading in the hearts" takes the form when a motive is found that does not allow speaking in favor of the opposite side. This technique can be combined not only with "stick arguments," but also with "smearing the argument." For example: "... your decency, excessive modesty, and false shame do not allow you to recognize this obvious fact and thereby support this progressive undertaking, on which the solution of the question, impatiently and hopefully expected by our voters, depends ...", etc...

17. Logical and psychological tricks

Their name is because, on the one hand, they can be built on violation of the laws of logic, and on the other, on the contrary, use formal logic to manipulate an object. Sophism was known in antiquity, requiring the answer "yes" or "no" to the question "have you stopped beating your father?" Any answer is difficult, because if the answer is "yes," then it means that he beat earlier, and if the answer is "no," then the object beats his father. There are many variants of such sophism: "... Do you all write denunciations?...", "... Have you already stopped drinking?..." etc. Public accusations are especially effective, and the main thing is to get a short answer and not allow a person to explain. The most common logical and psychological tricks include the conscious vagueness of the thesis put forward, or the answer to the question, when the idea is formulated vaguely, indefinitely, which allows it to be interpreted in different ways. In politics, this technique allows you to get out of difficult situations.

18. Failure to comply with the law is sufficient

Observance of the formal logical law of sufficient reason in discussions is very subjective because the participants in the discussion conclude the sufficient basis of the defended thesis. According to this law, arguments that are true and relevant to the thesis may be insufficient if they are private and do not provide grounds for conclusions. In addition to formal logic in the practice of information exchange, there is the so-called "Psycho-logic" (theory of argumentation), the essence of which is that argumentation does not exist on its own, it is put forward by certain people in certain conditions and perceived by concrete people who possess (or do not possess) certain knowledge, social status, personality qualities, etc. Therefore, a special case, elevated to the rank of regularity, often passes.

19. Change in emphasis in statements

In these cases, what the opponent said about the particular case is refuted as a general pattern. The reverse trick is that one or two facts are opposed to general reasoning, which in reality can be exceptions or atypical examples. Often, conclusions about the problem under discussion are made based on what "lies on the surface," for example, side effects of the development of a phenomenon.

20. Incomplete refutation

In this case, the combination of a logical violation with a psychological factor is used in those cases when they select the most vulnerable from the positions put forward by the opponent in their defense, break it down sharply and pretend that the other arguments do not even deserve attention. The trick passes if the opponent does not return to the topic.

21. The requirement of a clear answer

Using phrases like: "do not shirk ..", "say clearly, for all ...", "tell me directly ...", etc., the manipulation object is offered to give a definite answer "yes" or "no" to a question requiring a detailed answer or when the unambiguity of the answer can lead to a misunderstanding of the essence of the problem. In an audience with a low educational level, such a trick can be perceived as a manifestation of integrity, determination, and directness.

22. Artificial displacement of the dispute

In this case, having started discussing a situation, the manipulator tries not to give arguments, from which this statement follows, but suggests immediately proceeding to refute this. Thus, the possibility of criticizing one's position is limited, and the argument itself is shifted to the argumentation of the opposite side. If the opponent succumbed to this and begins to criticize the advanced position, giving various arguments, they try to argue around these arguments, looking for flaws in them, but not presenting their system of evidence for discussion.

23. "Multiple Questioning"

In the case of this manipulative reception, an object on the same topic is asked several different questions. They act depending on his answer: either they accuse him of not understanding the essence of the problem, or that he did not answer the question completely, or of trying to mislead.

- The eighth block of manipulations

Manipulative Effects Depending On The Type Of Behavior And Human Emotions

1. The first type. A person spends most of the time between a normal state of consciousness and a state of normal night sleep.

His upbringing, character, and habits control this type, and a sense of pleasure, a desire for security, and peace, i.e., all that is formed by verbal and emotionally-figurative memory. For most men of the first type, abstract mind, words, and logic prevail, and for most women of the first type, common sense, feelings, and fantasies prevail. Manipulative influence should be directed at the needs of such people.

2. The second type. The dominance of trance states.

These are super-suggestible and super-hypnotic people, whose behavior and reactions are controlled by the psychophysiology of the right hemisphere of the brain: imagination, illusions, dreams, dreamy desires, feelings, and sensations, belief in the unusual, faith in someone's authority, stereotypes, selfish or disinterested interests (conscious or unconscious), scenarios of events occurring with them, facts and circumstances. In the case of manipulative effects, it is recommended to influence such people's feelings and imagination.

3. The third type. The dominance of the left hemisphere of the brain.

Such people are controlled by verbal information and

principles, beliefs, and attitudes developed during a conscious analysis of reality. The external reactions of the third type are determined by their education and upbringing, as well as a critical and logical analysis of any information received from the outside world. To effectively influence them, it is necessary to reduce their analysis of the information presented to them by their left, critical, hemisphere of the brain. To do this, it is recommended to present information against the backdrop of trust in you. The information must be submitted strictly and carefully, using strictly logical conclusions, reinforce the facts exclusively with authoritative sources, appeal not to feelings and pleasures (instincts), but reason, conscience, duty, morality, justice, etc.

4. The fourth type. Primitive people with a predominance of cerebral instinctive-animal states.

In their main part, these are rude and uneducated people with an undeveloped left brain, who often grew up with mental retardation in socially dysfunctional families (alcoholics, prostitutes, drug addicts, etc.). Animal instincts and needs control such people's reactions and behavior: sexual instinct, the desire to eat well, sleep, drink, and experience more pleasant pleasures. When manipulating these people, it is necessary to influence the psychophysiology of the right brain: the previously experienced feelings, hereditary traits of behavior, stereotypes of behavior, the feelings that prevail at the moment, moods, fantasies, and instincts. It must be borne in mind that this category of people thinks primitively: if you satisfy their instincts and feelings, they respond positively.

5. The fifth type. People with an "expanded state of consciousness."

These are those who have managed to develop a highly spiritual person. In Japan, such people are called "enlightened," in India - "Mahatmas," in China - "perfect wise Tao people," in Russia - "holy prophets and miracle workers." Arabs of such people are called "holy Sufis." According to V.M. Kandyba, manipulators cannot influence such people, since they are "inferior to them in professional knowledge of man and nature."

6. The sixth type. People with a predominance of pathological conditions in their psychophysiology.

Mainly - mentally ill people. Their behavior and reactions are unpredictable, as they are abnormal. These people may perform some action due to a painful motive or being held captive by some hallucinations. Many of the people of this type become victims of totalitarian sects. Manipulations against such people must be carried out quickly and harshly, cause fear, a feeling of unbearable pain, isolation, and, if necessary, complete immobility and a special injection, depriving them of consciousness and activity.

7. The seventh type. People whose reactions and behavior are dominated by strong emotions are one or more of the basic underlying emotions, such as fear, pleasure, anger, etc.

Fear is one of the most powerful hypnogenic (generating hypnosis) emotions that always occurs in every person with a threat to his physical, social, or other well-being. Feeling fear, a person immediately falls into a narrowed, altered state of consciousness. The left brain is inhibited with its ability to the rational, critical-analytical, verbal-logical perception of what is happening, and the right brain is activated with its emotions, imagination, and instincts.

CHAPTER 7

IS THERE A MANIPULATIVE PERSON IN YOUR RELATIONSHIP?

Manipulative people do not hesitate to play termites in a romantic relationship, exerting financial or sexual pressure, sometimes displaying exaggerated kindness. To undermine your foundations, several scenarios are possible. Learn to recognize them!

Being in a relationship with a manipulative spouse or a manipulator is not that rare ...

Kindness: a calculated maneuver

"When pushed to the limit, I threatened to leave, Philippe became gentle as a lamb, adorable and very unhappy. I had the right to flowers, travel proposals. I felt a little guilty, not knowing better why I was leaving," says Patricia, 40, 2 children.

Signs of manipulation: his attitude is a very calculated maneuver. "Instead of questioning himself and hearing the change request, he deploys a strategy, with the sole objective of bringing you back," decodes psychotherapist Christel Petitcollin. When we take a close interest in their thought system, we can quickly realize that it has a fair rudimentary ready to think, based on binary logic. All or nothing, now or never, leave or stay. "Often impervious to criticism or questioning, they can make an effort only in the short term, to serve their interests," adds Sarah Serievic. What to do?

Above all, resist their injunction and stay in touch with your needs and requests for change. There is a good chance that the mask of kindness will pop off, reminding you very quickly of your desire to take your legs around your neck.

Money: constant pressure

"My husband and I have a good situation. Yet after shopping for several purchases, I hide them in the closet and show off a new one every three days. I feel spied on and fear that he calls me a spendthrift petty bourgeoisie, always in the tone of mockery, of course." Monique, 43 years old.

Signs of manipulation: "Manipulators often manage to make their victim live in an artificial financial shortage," remarked Christel Petitcollin during his consultations. Regardless of the amount of your income, you always have the diffuse feeling of being a budget gourd. You flirt more often than before with overdrafts. "In reality, the financial manipulation is real," reports Isabelle Nazare-Aga, behavioral therapist. He can forget his credit card at the restaurant, or make you believe that the distribution of charges is fair while you pay for groceries, school supplies, and half the rent ... And he just gas and gasoline.

What to do? This financial aspect often works against you. At the risk of sounding like a lie, do the accounts of who pays what, and adjust! If he refuses, you will be fixed on his bad faith and the decision to be made.

Sexuality: a misplaced requirement

"Receiving waves of coarse words whispered in my ear ... Caressing myself with a sex toy in front of him ... Sexually, I often felt uncomfortable. I didn't know how far I should go or not to satisfy him," admits Sylvie, 33 years old.

Signs of manipulation: Exploring new lands in terms of sexuality is always possible, as long as you feel particularly confident and respected. "A climate that does not create a manipulator who will not hesitate to spice up his lovemaking, especially to test your obedience," points out Christel Petitcollin. It is often a refusal in the face of sexual practice or a certain frequency that will make him obsessive. From there to feeling "stuck," there is only one step!

Conversely, Sarah Serievic underlines that "in manipulative women, abstinence, on the contrary, is often a means of pressure."

What to do? Going beyond your limits to "have peace" will not change anything. The manipulator will make a "fixette" on something else. Know yourself and respect yourself so that you can say no if you need to.

Communication: a great complexity

"I find it hard to communicate with my husband. The conversation is disjointed; he changes the subject, finishes the sentences for me. I have the impression that I can no longer think for myself, that I am struggling to keep track of my thoughts, "says Emmanuelle, 37.

Signs of manipulation: Manipulators seek to confuse rather than clarify. They jump from rooster to donkey, use ambiguous information, deliver half-truths. In reality, it confuses you, creates digressions, and ends these sentences with a "You see what I mean." But why? "Blurring the tracks, not taking responsibility for their words, are all means that the manipulators use to keep control within the couple" answers Christel Petitcollin.

What to do? Don't be fooled. Behind their communication's false complexity, remember that they are often immature, and intellectually lazy, their vocabulary is limited.

Manipulation and grip relationships

Getting out of a relationship of manipulation and control is not an easy thing. The first step to take is also the most difficult: to start and realize that there is a problem.

Mechanisms involved

The manipulation and the grip rest essentially on using three feelings: fear, doubt, and guilt, to establish a relationship of dependence.

Manipulators use mainly four techniques:

The seduction: The person flatters you, compliments you; you are physically and intellectually attracted, you touch, you door attention, and your values.

The victimization: If she has a problem with other people, she will always consider that it is the fault of others: people are wicked, people do her harm, she can not help because she is the victim.

Bullying: It can be physical, emotional, financial, etc. The manipulator can threaten explicitly or implicitly to harm you and withdraw your affection, support, or anything else.

The guilt: Another side of victimization is the person under the influence who is accused of being responsible for the current state, the discomfort, the problems the person is handling.

The classic path is:

Seduction phase

The manipulator undermines the foundation of a person's balance (his or her values, he or she pulls on the sensitive chord, hits on the sensitive points, instills doubt in oneself and others).

The victim's isolation from his usual social environment, his family, his friends, his supporters. It can cause you to be suspicious or hurt your loved ones.

Establishment of dependency: the manipulative person has done you a service, helps you, gives you (attention, affection, services, compliments, gifts, etc.), then takes it back or turns off the tap, leaving you frustrated. It is this frustration, combined with the habit of her presence and her position of a savior, that she will use to confirm your dependence on her. She will change the rules, remind you that she has helped you a lot, that it is thanks to her that you have been able to succeed or accomplish such and such a thing, she will pretend that she wants your good, that she knows that which is good for you, to take control of your life.

How to get out

When in doubt: distance yourself. Move away from the

person for a while, switch off the ignition, and take this time to listen to yourself, your feelings, your emotions. If you feel better and think that indeed the person with whom you were in contact was manipulating you or trying to get you under control, it will be necessary to completely and definitively break the link to protect yourself.

Do not try to help the manipulative person, and it is not your role. Your role is to protect yourself above all.

The older and longer the hold, the more difficult it is to move away and realize the manipulation. Over time, the victim of influence feels less and less capable and more and more isolated and impoverished since there is dependence and sabotage of the foundations of the victim and of other relationships that he could maintain.

After getting out of the relationship, it will take some time to rebuild: reconnect with your values, friends, family, find safety, mourn the relationship, express your emotions; turn to history, shed new light and a new look on it that will allow you to understand and put into words what happened, and turn the page. Kindness with oneself is a key ingredient in this process of reconstruction. A professional aid worker (psychiatrist, psychologist, psychopractor, or other) can support you in this psychological reconstruction process thanks to various tools (cognitive-behavioral therapies, active and empathetic listening, relaxation, personal development tools, and self-esteem, etc.).

In a relationship, do not accept "neither seduction nor aggression" (Jacques Salomé, ESPERE method) and remember to research your feelings and your emotions regularly. This will decrease the chances of falling under the influence of a narcissistic pervert or a pathological manipulator.

Remember that you deserve to be respected, loved as you are, and not to be used.

In love, do not let yourself be manipulated!

A relationship is normally based on trust, exchange, and respect. However, the spouse can sometimes instill guilt, devalue, sow discord ... In short, try to manipulate you! So how do you regain self-confidence when your lover turns out to be an emotional vampire?

"We live together, and we are not happy. Initially, everything is going well, and then day after day, the situation deteriorates ..." Nothing to do with the routine that can settle in a relationship. No, sometimes, these are real toxic relationships!

What to do when your spouse devalues you and makes you feel guilty, to manipulate you ultimately? "Prolonged contact generates feelings of aggression, fear, or sadness," says Isabelle Nazare-Aga, behavior therapist. Without separating, learn how to get over it and assert yourself in your relationship! The strategy is simple: identify the type of manipulative spouse, then protect yourself from this relational scourge.

The manipulator denigrates you without your knowledge.

He chooses you as his partner, and yet it is crazy how easy

it is to say bad things about you, casually, to your friends. "Frederique, a cordon bleu, you must be kidding." The manipulative spouse bombards you with criticism, which undermines your self-confidence.

The Shrink's Opinion:

You find these reflections harmless. In reality, it is not the occasional scratch in your self-esteem that is dangerous, but the frequency of negative messages. To upgrade yourself, cultivate your professional environment skills, for example, far from its grip.

The manipulator isolates you from the rest of society.

He purrs at the thought of seeing you slaving away at work. But he is capricious if you show independence, like accepting an invitation (to dinner, to the theater, on weekends), without him. His thinking system requires that any free moment from one must be given to the other.

The Shrink's Opinion:

Your discomfort is diffuse, and you feel divided. As soon as you practice an activity without him, you feel guilty. If you give in to him, you are very frustrated. Position yourself without delay. Make the point that your desires are as valuable as his.

The manipulator is devouring jealousy.

He aspires to an exclusive relationship and does not suffer any possible "competitor." But the manipulator can practice a double game. In the evenings, his seductive number with the opposite sex frequently rubs his jealousy towards those who approach you.

The Shrink's Opinion:

You experience recurring scenes where he searches for evidence of your infidelity. Adopt the fog tactics: above all, do not start a showdown with him, you will only multiply his animosity. Just act surprised without actually arguing.

The manipulator preaches the false to know the truth.

Communication with him takes on the appearance of a difficult path. All pretexts are good to sow confusion. So he manages to ask a question including an erroneous element: Did you know that Eric had a mistress?

The Shrink's Opinion:

If your friend just falls, you may be in trouble. Try to hide your emotion and decode his words' underlying meaning (facial expressions, tone of voice, looks). It is exhausting but radical to distinguish between true and false.

CHAPTER 8

SUBDUING THE MIND

The computer that drives your mind, body, and soul, is your subconscious mind. This takes direction from your mind's conscious part and then carries out its function – to the letter. Who we are, what we do, and how we act are all down to the fact that we have no conscience? Imagine the power that is so immaterial that no modern computer can sense it. It is our cerebral cortex's spirit, the divine cord, which guides us in our life. What if I said you could train your subconscious mind and concentrate on making massive success?

You may. You can. Worldwide, people apply science or more mystical approaches to open the iron doors to the conscious mind and put their delicate hands on the subconscious. You change the threads that make you who you are— a reprogramming. A whole lifetime of conditioning is up against you. You can reprogram and rebuild your subconscious with the right techniques and application until it becomes a natural part of your life.

Have you ever seen somebody who likes to say, "I think you don't like to do that, subconsciously?" Regardless of how hard you try, you seem to be recoiling, constructing, and distaste progressive inertia. It can be changed; you can transform your entire attitude and make life much easier and meaningful.

By now, you could be wondering, how do I do this? Many approaches are available on the market, and many businesses specialize in deep brain stimulation. The key is to trick and subdue the mind to a profound trance, relax the mind, and shorten the normal defenses. When this is achieved, the subconscious becomes more malleable, and reprogramming can then begin. Breathing is very important here, and some businesses use that to build a sense of peace and glide the individual into a profoundly meditative state by using a screened floating tank.

This technology powers medical studies into Parkinson's disease healing or amnesia and dementia healing. It has also been extensively researched and used as an aid to improve the care of chronic patients and promote better prosperity. The mind state is a strong thing, and it can change universes within us. Just a few areas can be investigated with applied technologies, such as magnetic fields and sound frequencies for cortical stimulation.

Next time it is quite likely that you don't need aspirin if you have a headache. It's just the state of your mind that you could only alter. With a mind that thinks nothing can't be solved, almost any problem can be slowly eroded or strengthened.

Quieting the Mind and Being Present

The language of the heart is intuition. Intuition. Our intuition is mainly a self-speech. It also uses other methods of communication, but intuition serves as the ideas for the heart. Intuition almost constantly flows like thoughts, but it takes some time to be mindful of intuitions because they are much more subtle than thoughts. Thoughts normally get our attention over intuitions for that reason.

One of the advantages of meditation and other spiritual practices that suppress the selfish mind is that these practices offer more insight. Many need meditation or other spiritual practices to subdue the dominance of the egoistic mind. Once a certain superiority of the egoic intellect is reached, real progress towards our intuition can be made.

The egoistic mental is quiet because it keeps the mind occupied with a task by meditation or other activity that concentrates the mental mind. Any activity in which we fully participate can be a meditation. The mind is quiet and serves us only where needed if we focus all our attention on anything.

We tend not to dive into and experience the moment but to get by on life's surface. The egoic mind keeps us a long way off the real experience and replaces thoughts on it. It takes us away from now when life is full and living. By just realizing what's going on, we can be more aware at this time. Being more present usually takes away our thoughts and feelings and puts them on whatever else happens.

Exercise: Being Present

To be present is to reflect on all that is happening at present, not only your thoughts or feelings. If a thought comes into being, consider it, and then start to observe all else. When you do a job, and your mind wanders away, bring back your attention to the task, the current stimuli, and the experience. Through practice, it will become more normal to be involved in everything that is happening right now.

Another effective method is to do a more formal kind of meditation. Meditation regularly makes the intuition and, therefore, the guidance of the self more accessible and helps to establish a calm state of mind. Meditation is the most effective spiritual method available for moving into the experience of our true nature from the egoistic state of consciousness. It is neither more difficult nor complicated than being involved in a sport.

Exercise: Sitting in Meditation

Engage in meditating every day, even if for only a few minutes a day. Start with 10 minutes a day of meditation. Increase the time you meditate with rising pleasure. Make your meditation experience as comfortable, pleasant, and enjoyable as possible, so you look forward to meditation.

Come back to a calm place. Choose something that you want to concentrate on so you can enjoy your meditation. You might like to hear music or sounds in your room if you are auditory. If you are kinesthetic, you would likely like to focus on physical feelings and subtle energy sensations. You might like to look at a holy picture, a work of art, colors, flowers, or anything of nature if you are more visual.

Return it to what you concentrate on, whenever your mind wanders. Notice also what you feel while sitting in meditation. The experience is still happening, while the mind is busy with what it is focusing on. That's what you are, that experience! When you practice more meditation, your mind wanders less and less, and you spend more and more time in the moment.

As soon as you start to spend more time, meditation is extremely pleasant. It's now extremely enjoyable. It has all: joy, happiness, peace, enjoyment, success, devotion, insight, and wisdom. You're going to be asking if you ever had a stroll, but you're going to catch up again. The ego-mind, though the present is so cheerful and pure, is very seductive. Even those who primarily live in today are still roaming through the halls of the egoic mind.

We should learn to be present in our selfish thinking just as we are present to anything else that may arise. The idea may be like all other things that we also have. We don't feel like we worry about our feelings when we are present to them, but rather as we know that they are thought, which is very different from our normal thinking. This is a workout that helps you to learn to be present to your thoughts:

Exercise: Being Present to Thoughts

If you practice your thinking, your relationship will change to learning. As ideas emerge, practice as much as possible.

Right now, notice what thinking is emerging. Look at it as if you were at a distance. What's the thought experience? Notice that thought appears to be in your head. What is thought-conscious? Do you have even the consciousness of your body? What is the size? Is it a frontier? What is this perception experience? That's the one you are. You are aware of the coming and going emotions.

The theories that emerge in your narcissistic mind are irrelevant to who you are. It's not up to you what comes into your selfish mind. You've only been given the conditioning. Without thinking, reflecting on your thinking, or keeping an opinion on thinking, simply observe how your thoughts come and go. From where will they come? Where do they go? Where are they going? Notice the lack of coherence between thoughts and how they jump from one thing to another. Often, it seems that they are designed exclusively for you. What else are you noticing? Are they tied up with different voices? Are you aware of certain subjects? What's their truth? Have they an influence on consciousness?

This way, we can be rational about thought. Being present to thinking. We should look at our feelings with objectivity so that it was not true when we were associated with them. During this test, much about our conditioning's essence can be discovered, and we can liberate ourselves from that awareness of our conditioning.

This new connection to the greedy mind is highly open. It can free us and allow us to understand the fullness of the moment. Based on the absence of the selfish mind's influence to define us, we are free to pay attention not only to our thoughts but also to our entire life. We find that part and parcel of what happens throughout life is that through intuition, the Self speaks to us.

CHAPTER 9

WHAT IS DARK NLP?

Neuro-Linguistic Programming (NLP) is a methodology focused on how our internal, mental and emotional processes work. Especially on the influence that language has on our mental programming and other functions of our nervous system.

NLP asks how we do what we do and the relationship between our behaviors and our experiences. It teaches us to "reprogram" (program) our minds using language (linguistics), which encodes the experience perceived by the neurological (neuro) system, to have successful results in any area of our lives.

NLP offers techniques for overcoming limitations, generating positive internal states, increasing self-confidence, unlocking emotional brakes, changing habits, influential communication, curing phobias, improving relationships, eliminating limiting beliefs ... It is a method that offers a healthy and positive way of communicating with the environment and with oneself.

NLP SESSIONS

NLP sessions are normally called NLP therapy because NLP is an effective communication model. This learning process trains people to increase awareness of the perception of their reality and to be able to change it. This process is very fast and effective because NLP has specific techniques to access the "files" that the client has engraved in their minds and provides the "updates" necessary to change the emotional response associated with the problem. These changes are lasting and profound because the client learns to use new strategies and behavior patterns to overcome fears, improve relationships, and resolve conflicts.

What is NLP for? Who is it for? What areas of action are required?

Neuro-Linguistic Programming is currently a valuable area of knowledge that provides techniques to improve communication with others and with oneself. By focusing on understanding internal processes, it provides control over what we feel and do and makes us more effective in any area of our life.

NLP to change habits

NLP has created specific techniques to change habits. A habit is a behavior for which hardly any effort or concentration is needed, and that is generated after repeating it for a time. One of the conditions that define a habit is that it is learned and not innate behavior.

NLP is well known for having a high percentage of success in treating harmful habits such as smoking, nail-biting, overeating ... The model of change of habits that Anna Flores applies includes an NLP technique that associates it with something unpleasant than to fix the process with an Ericksonian hypnosis exercise, installing in the unconscious the freedom to no longer depend on the habit.

NLP for emotional management

NLP achieves very good results in relatively short periods in emotional management. NLP asks us how we do what we do, how we "archive" experience in the brain, and how we respond to it, so we can change it. When a client wants to improve some aspect of his life whose emotional response does not satisfy him, there is no change in the situation or the environment. The change consists in the way the client perceives it; that is, it changes his emotional response.

These are some of the objectives most demanded by clients:

- Increased self-esteem
- Increased security and self-confidence
- Stress reduction
- Improving social skills
- Overcoming trauma
- Develop communication skills
- Increased concentration in studies or work
- Management of specific crises: divorce, dismissal, exams...
- Cure of phobias: insects, reptiles, fear of flying, fear of heights...

NLP for athletes

Neuro-Linguistic Programming gives excellent results in the world of sports; in fact, elite athletes use NLP techniques to generate an internal state so powerful that it helps them to program success. It is widely demonstrated that mood, mental concentration, and positive beliefs greatly influence the achievement of sports goals and that, often, these elements make the difference between a mediocre athlete and an excellent one.

It provides a new way of maintaining the attitude of success in the practice of the sport.

It provides internal security and trust tools to ensure success consistently and unconsciously.

It teaches mastery of space, body movements, sensations, and emotions to produce high performance.

Key points of NLP

- Increases awareness of own abilities
- Focuses on the solution, not the problem
- Provides new behavioral options
- It teaches flexibility of behavior
- Improves communication with others and with oneself

The ten Effective NLP Techniques

The most widely used NLP techniques are rapport, covert orders, anchorage, body physiology, eye access, external or internal reference, belief changes, and alternative illusion. In this chapter, we will explain them in detail.

Neuro-linguistic programming is a work methodology created in 1970 by Richard Bandler (computer scientist and psychologist) and John Grinder (linguist) in which they combine communication, personal development, and psychotherapy.

This approach seeks to achieve more self-knowledge, enhance contact with others, and inspire people to adapt and reach their goals. Research by the writers has shown that changes in psychiatric conditions like depression, phobia, psychosomatic problems, and learning disabilities can be made in the NLP ...

The authors of the NLP were Virginia Satir, Milton Erickson, Fritz Perls, Gregory Batson, Alfred Korzybski, or Noam Chomsky.

 One of them was Bandler and Grinder. In their research, these two scholars explore how neural mechanisms, language, and the spectrum of learned behaviors relate to each other. The latter can be changed to achieve the goals each person has in his or her life.

Therefore, Bandler and Grinder affirm that the NLP methodology can model people's skills until they achieve their aims. More recent scientist work has subsequently debunked the idea that all such issues can be solved.

However, the reality is that today it continues to be used in multiple areas such as emotion management, leadership, the development of creativity, the increase in communication, and the educational field.

Also, it has been used in psychology, personal development in general, commerce to promote sales, motivation in sports, and companies at both the individual and group levels.

Where does the name neurolinguistic programming

come from?

Neurolinguistic programming owes its name to the relationship of 3 aspects of the human being that come together in this methodology:

Program

In Nitrolingual programming methodology. Similar to machines, our brain is a device. Mental programs coordinate our knowledge. Thus, these mental programs direct our actions to achieve our goals.

Neuro

All learning requires a neural network to carry out and store the learning in the short or long term. The human being develops his understanding of his experiences and everything around him through the nervous system.

The language

The latter term is based on NLP. For our interactions and learning, language is important to connect with others.

Ten professional NLP

NLP strategies help break out of the well-known comfort zone for all those who need a guide to conquer challenges and are resistant to change.

These are intended to provide you with the means required, but it is important to make the change and believe that it is feasible and beneficial to achieve it.

When you pursue your goals, your well-being will rise. The

more energy you use in NLP's resources, the more likely the success will be. These tools are designed to be used to better your daily life.

First, I'll clarify the most commonly used NLP techniques.

Study

This strategy is used when we want to improve our contact with people, whether at work or in the community.

This seeks to establish a culture of collaboration and confidence in which there are no malentenduities, debates, or judgments. It is also possible to grasp the message that the other person wants to transmit and convey the message that we want to transmit to the listener.

We take advantage of the listing of things we know that connect us with our listener. The relationship is vitally essential in addition to the use of verbal words.

Covers orders

The questions are usually formulated according to this technique and finish with an ascending musical intonation, while the orders are made with a descending intonation.

Thus, NLP provides the desired effect to tone the questions in descending order.

Mooring

Anchoring in a stressful situation is a technique to lessen an emotion of discomfort such as anxiety or anguish. It is based on the classical conditioning of learning psychology.

Physiology

They need to learn how the body works and how posture, breathing styles, and the heart rate affect our attitudes and emotions, among others.

As we adjust our body posture and learn to air correctly, we will alter our comportment and, hence, communicate well in other countries.

Entry to the eyes

The eye accesses are part of physiology, and they refer to the fact that the eye motion sequence corresponds to the person's purpose.

External or reference standard

References are a form of a mental model, unconscious and systemic.

Being conscious of both ours and other patterns helps us to build self-knowledge and empathy for others.

In particular, the reference standard allows us to know on which of our behaviors they based their requirements and value levels. This is where our decision-making process will reside.

Two comparison types can be distinguished:

External guide: People use this tool to reflect on their thoughts and feelings in the world. We would use topics such as how we feel about decision-taking and how we want to affect their opinion.

External reference: Individuals with this form of reference put great importance on others' views and are searching for agreement with the others around them. The sentences we use will expose our views since the person will consider them (e.g., My view is that...).

Audio / visual / kinesthetic

The person has different choices (visual, auditory, or kinesthetic) for decision-making.

We're going to use this to imply, for example, our target if we are going to convince a person whose preferred medium is auditory ("I'll tell you about the travel plan I prepared").

It is changing in values and personality strength

If we can identify our present beliefs, internally disputed ideas, and change in them on the basis that beliefs determine our situation, we can change our situation.

An alternative illusion

This strategy is designed to convince others to do what we want. There are several options for the person to choose from, but everyone is geared to what we want to achieve.

For example, we would ask you to reach the beach by car or train, if our goal is to reach the beach. Or won't you go to the beach instead?

Possibility or requirement modal operators

According to NLP, metaprograms are solid, unconscious thought techniques for people. These include modal operators in the form of implicit instructions for our internal dialogs of the possibility or need.

These implicit orders are expressed in the form of words; I need, need, need, etc. Each one produces a person's emotions.

So that it can be better understood, here is a practical example. It is very common to use the sentence: "I can't" to excuse failure, and the question we always come back with is, why can't you?

The person will give an infinite list of reasons if we return the question of why he cannot perform the actions. If the question is, on the other hand, "What stops you?" we direct the individual, instead of thinking about excuses, to consider possible solutions to their problem. In other words, the emphasis is on the solution.

Exercise realistic

First, the NLP technique is being developed to increase motivating strategies to achieve a goal or condition.

We begin to think of something that motivates us to do a great deal. Imagine a film that takes place and knows the strengths of this action, which takes all its specifics into account. Terminate activity and relax.

See and breathe deeply around you. Then think of something that you don't want to, pay close attention to what you hear.

See the picture and its qualities. Rest again, and take a deep breath. Compare activities or pictures, focusing on all of your details. Write down a list of motivational elements in this process.

Finally, you should take a picture that belongs to a pleasant and varying visual characteristic, size, distance, movement, etc.

Of all the changes that have been made, stick to the combination of qualities that make you happier and more inspiring. Write them down so that you can use them later for a motivational scenario.

Benefits from NLP use

The methods used in NLP provide several advantages that cover a broad range of needs and objectives that anyone can consider at some stage in their life.

Build knowledge of oneself

Emotional management: in any situation, a person should control and manage emotions and actions (such as being able to effectively face a job interview).

Through our communication techniques, NLP uses anchors to achieve goals or solve problems when dealing with stressful situations. One of the most common issues in the field of communication is the fear of publicity. This usually gives rise to fear and anguish. Through the anchoring strategy, an enjoyable, comfortable, and optimistic time that we recall is "anchored" and is correlated with the stressful situation at the exact moment using visualization techniques.

Learn strategies for innovation

Improve motivation strategies: improve motivation strategies and make them more effective in the achievement of personal or professional goals.

Understand our and others' learning styles: our questions are often guided by lessons that have been learned over time. Associations of experiences and contexts have produced a pattern of thought because they have occurred again and again and are hard to modify.

Enhance our ability to achieve personal goals: reasons concealed in the unconscious and that necessarily promote delay in achieving our goals. This involves identifying and understanding the reason so that subsequent adjustments can take place and decisions to take action.

Develop effective strategies for decision-making

Understand, embrace, and learn how to manage cycles of personal and professional transition.

Remove phobias and fears.

CHAPTER 10

COMMUNICATE WITH NLP

Neuro-Linguistic Programming (NLP) is an approach developed in the 1970s in the United States by Richard Bandler, computer scientist and psychologist, and John Grinder, linguist and psychologist. They observed how well-known and valued communicators went about being efficient. Their thesis is based on the idea that if we can identify how a person goes about succeeding by decoding his "program," we can use it to succeed.

The "program" in question here reproduces the attitudes and behaviors, what the person thinks when he acts, his emotions, the values that guide him, and the objectives he pursues.

In terms of communication, we are effective when we can make ourselves understood, and when this communication leads to action. This is true when the interlocutors find interest and desire to maintain the relationship.

The effectiveness of communication, therefore, does not lie in its intention, but the results obtained. We communicate to share facts, feelings, values , and above all, to influence others.

Five principles for excellent communication

According to NLP, there are levers for developing excellent communication, including the following five principles:

- Pursue a defined and precise objective
- Create a quality relationship right away
- Pay attention to your interlocutor
- Adapt flexibly
- Stay consistent and relevant

1 / Pursue a defined and precise objective

Before starting communication, you should know in advance what you want. Is it to inform, to convince, to be appreciated? Before starting a meeting, an interview, and memo, it helps to ask yourself: "What do I want to achieve?" If, for example, you have a long e-mail to write, a report or an article to write for the job, it is recommended that you start with the conclusion first, before preparing the outline and content of the message.

If you want information from a seller about a state-of-the-art flat screen, advertise your goal. If you want to go on vacation in August, say so. You will thus avoid the risk of manipulating or entering into a situation of incomprehension. Encourage your interlocutors also to express their objectives clearly as quickly as possible.

2 / Create a quality relationship straight away

The popular adage: "It's the first impression that counts" holds in communication. If you create an unpleasant atmosphere for your interlocutors from the start of the meeting, they will not want to listen to you, much less to dialogue with you. Some communicators recommend applying the "eighty" rule. They know they have little time to catch the attention of their interlocutors.

What is this "eighty" rule? The first twenty seconds, the first twenty words, the first twenty gestures, the first twenty steps, and the twenty square centimeters of the face.

For example, if at a meeting you start your speech hesitantly, looking at the ground, the scowl, using words like "we can try to," "maybe," " ... ", you risk creating an atmosphere of doubt, apathy, or demotivation.

On the contrary, if you address your audience with active terms, looking at your interlocutors and accompanying your words with opening gestures, you will immediately capture your audience's attention.

3 / Pay attention to your interlocutor

When you talk to people, focus your attention on them. You will notice their attitudes of agreement, disapproval, or doubt. For example, when a person says "yes" to you, they can very well mean "no" with the tone of their voice, the movements of their head, and their shoulders. A mother knows very quickly when her child tells her a lie.

Focusing your attention also means listening to the comments and fears of your interlocutors. There is nothing more eloquent than someone who says nothing.

4 / Adapt flexibly

In communication, what matters are results, not intentions. The best-orchestrated arguments may be incomprehensible to your audience. You may be right on the merits; if your words offend or scare others, they do not want to listen. In these cases, with your sense of observation, change your arguments. To persist, repeating the same arguments, would be equivalent to sinking yourself even further into error. Experience is sometimes a way of repeating the same mistakes more quickly. Parents who get angry with their children during evening homework at home understand this impasse. The hardest part is finding another communication strategy. "To learn Latin at Luculus, you have to know Latin, Luculus, and especially the method adapted to Luculus."

5 / Stay consistent and relevant

How many changes fail because of the gulf between saying it and doing?

Take the example of a leader who advocates responsiveness and flexibility and signs the letter in eight days. When you give a compliment, have a smiley face. When you issue an objection, accompany your statements with an appropriate gesture, without displaying an ironic smile. When you want to get an important message across, you can spoil your effect by saying, "I have a little talk to you."

The presentation of these five principles could imply that they occur in chronological order: first, have a specific objective, create the relationship, etc. In practice, these five criteria also apply simultaneously.

The state of mind first!

To learn and apply NLP tools, let us emphasize that the state of mind is just as important as the method itself, and it is based on five hypotheses:

- We know a lot more than we think we know. We have within us the necessary resources to carry out our existence.
- The more choices we have, the more efficient we are. Choosing is a mark of freedom.
- We cannot communicate; we only communicate.
- What we believe to be reality is, in fact, only our interpretation of this reality through our filters, and judgments.
- What validates the effectiveness of communication is not the intention but the result.

To communicate well with others, listen to them, accept that they have other convictions than yours, find acceptable compromises to live and work together. Be open to others, even if it means making mistakes. These technical blunders are preferable to negative intentions in the service of manipulation and abuse of power.

NLP presuppositions

Getting your messages across and making yourself understood requires relevant communication tools. This is what NLP (Neuro-Linguistic Programming) offers models and techniques to learn to communicate more effectively, be successful and faster, and change easily. It is based on fundamental postulates, the presuppositions which we describe below.

1. The map is not the territory

This notion corresponds to the fact that we perceive the world (the territory) through our five senses. We make an internal representation of it (the map), which is not exactly the reality. Therefore, each of us has our world map, and there is no map better than another.

2. A positive purpose accompanies every behavior

The good intent determines all behavior. It means giving them a sense of quality if a manager's employees are too demanding for example. He does it for his employees' benefit, in his opinion.

Intending rather than a description of "problem" actions may be simpler and more productive. The question is: what could the good motive behind the other's actions be?

3. You can't communicate

In the morning, you are lost in thought, and you meet a colleague without saying hello. You did not have an intention towards him but receive a message from him. The words (the verbal) represent only 7% of the message, speaking (the para verbal), and the non-verbal represent the remaining 92%! In the presence of the other, even if we do not intend to communicate, we communicate anyway.

Since individuals cannot help but influence each other, a good question to ask is: to what extent am I helping maintain this situation?

4. We are not our behaviors

It is useful to distinguish a person's identity from their behavior. Indeed, while it is relatively easy to help a person change their behavior, it is impossible to change their nature. It's about changing problematic behavior while respecting the person.

5. Body and mind interact

What happens in the mind has repercussions in the body, and vice versa. If we observe the modifications of the non-verbal, we can deduce concomitant modifications at the level of thought.

6. It is possible to reproduce the performance of others

The NLP designers studied the behaviors of excellent therapists and deduced techniques to reproduce their performances and generalize them. In NLP, it is therefore considered that it is possible to reproduce and model individuals' effective behaviors.

7. The meaning of what we communicate is in the response we get

Have you ever met someone's eyes without any particular intention, and yet this person gives you a black look or even invective? Even if you are unaware of what you are communicating, you get a response that matters.

Therefore, it is important to assess how the message is understood and, if so, how to change it to aim for more efficiency. It is about being receptive to the impact of your messages (feedback) and taking it into account to adjust your communication to the model of the world of your interlocutor.

8. The more choices, the better

At a given time, people adopt the best possible choice, taking into account their possibilities and capacities and according to what they perceive to be valid for them in their world model.

It is the variety of choices that makes it possible to face the complexity of a situation, and which allows that, when it does not work, we can change the way we do it, and therefore try something else. One of the NLP goals is to give people more options, more choices, and make them more flexible.

9. Each person has all the resources to get what they want

Each individual has within him the resources to obtain what he desires. You just have to teach him how to use them or discover them. This presupposition invites everyone to regain power over their lives. It considers that a person's limits are only the representation he makes of them.

10. There is no such thing as failure, and there is only feedback

While failure and error can make you feel guilty and demotivated, viewing an unexpected response as feedback from a context empowers and invites action: a different outcome than the desired one is to consider additional information about how we are doing.

11. If you don't achieve your goal with a behavior, change that behavior

When you can't reach a goal, try something else. One of the basics of NLP is flexibility.

What assumptions do you want to use?

CHAPTER 11

HOW TO USE DARK SEDUCTION IN YOUR LIFE

The dark side of seduction: how to prevent progress with women from bringing you more unhappiness.

In this chapter, we focus on a very important topic for all those who are on the path of improving skills with women, especially aimed at those who are just taking their first steps and also those who already have enough experience with women but still feel very unhappy.

I want to talk about what I call "the dark side of seduction." By this, I mean when our progress at the social level and with women brings us more suffering and unhappiness instead of giving us that feeling of confidence and happiness that we seek to achieve.

What we all look for when improving skills with women

Almost all of us who seek to consciously improve our skills with women look for one specific thing. At first, our main reason is sex. We are motivated by the need to have as much sex as possible with women.

But deep down, we all have a deeper motivation that is difficult to detect during our early years of progress with women. Beyond seeking to have as much sex as possible with as many women as possible, deep down, our greatest motivation is to feel secure in ourselves and feel happy.

In other words, we seek confidence and happiness. At a superficial level, what motivates us to improve skills with women is sex, but at a deep level, what motivates us is to reach a point where we feel confident and happy. Beyond sex, what motivates almost all of us who seek progress with women are those two things: trust and happiness.

Our biggest dream with women

So, almost all of us embarked on this path, dreaming of obtaining those three things: sex, trust, and happiness. We assume that when we start to get the experiences and results that we seek with women, we will get those three things.

We assume that when we start having enough sex with many women and have one or more girlfriends, we will feel confident and happy. That is the great dream of almost all of us who embark on this path of progress with women.

Now, the problem is that perfecting your skills with women will give you the ability to have more sex, but it will not increase your confidence or happiness. Becoming more skillful on a social level will allow you to achieve all your goals with women. You are going to be able to get the amount of sex you want, you are going to get the type of women you want, and you will get the girlfriends you are looking for. But all those results are not going to bring you confidence or happiness.

I know this is difficult to accept, especially if you are

starting. If you are taking your first steps and do not believe in what I just told you, then I do not blame you because many find it difficult to believe.

So if you do not believe it, what I recommend is that you ignore what I just told you and go out with everything to get the results you are looking for and check for yourself if it is true or not.

Improve your skills with women if it is going to give you the ability to get all the sex you want. Even your results are going to make you feel confident and happy in the short term. For example, during a night when you conquer a very hot woman, you will feel very confident and happy. The next day after having sex with her, you will feel very confident and very happy.

But after a few days, that feeling will disappear, and you will again feel a kind of emptiness as if something is missing. That feeling of confidence and happiness you get from having sex with her will start to diminish until you return to your natural state.

In the long term, the results with women will not give you the confidence and happiness you are looking for. As I said before, I know that this is very shocking to hear for those who are starting because it goes against that initial dream that we all have to find confidence and happiness in our achievements with women. It is normal that when someone tells us something that goes against our dreams, we close ourselves.

But I mention it because it is important to know, especially from the beginning so as not to fall into the "dark side" of which I will speak later in this chapter.

The two stages of growth: strengthening the ego and letting go

To explain what I mean by falling into "the dark side of seduction," I must first outline something very important. This idea is one of the greatest discoveries made in these years of progress. It is extremely valuable because it offers you a lot of perspectives to grow healthily and not get lost along the way.

The process of personal growth has two stages:

Strengthen the ego

Before talking about this stage, I want to clarify what the ego is. The ego is your mind. Thanks to having a mind, you can identify yourself as an entity of your own and separate from others. Thanks to having a mind, you can say, "this is me, these are my thoughts, emotions, and actions."

Now the ego is not bad. Within personal growth, the ego is often spoken of as something evil and disastrous. The truth is that it is not bad; it is extremely necessary to evolve as people. Without the ego, that is, without the mind, we could not grow personally. The problem is when we become attached to the ego, and we will talk about that later.

So this stage of growth is to strengthen your ego (your mind). When I refer to "strengthen," I mean progress and growth. There are many ways to strengthen the ego, but the main ones are:

- Acquire new knowledge
- Acquire new experiences
- Acquire new skills
- Face emotional challenges

When we acquire new knowledge, experience, skills, or face emotional challenges, we provide the necessary stimulus to our minds to grow. This type of stimuli strengthens us, and makes us grow mentally. It is as if our mind is a computer, and we are updating it to a new version when we provide these stimuli.

In seduction, we strengthen the ego when we educate ourselves on the subject, for example, we read an article, watch a video, buy a book, or buy a course. When we acquire new experiences with women, for example, we manage to have sex with a woman that we like the same night.

But above all, our ego is strengthened when we improve our skills and face emotional challenges. That is why it is very important to constantly go out as it is the only way to improve skills. Going out once in a while can bring you new experiences, but it won't improve your skills much. On the other hand, when you constantly go out, your skills improve a lot, and you gain a lot of emotional strength thanks to frequently facing all the great fears that arise when meeting new women.

So when you get an education, new experiences, and when you constantly go out to improve your skills with women, you are strengthening your ego. You are growing mentally, and you are becoming more efficient. This stage of growth is what we all know. Now let's look at the other stage, which almost everyone ignores.

Let go

This stage consists of disidentifying yourself from your ego. In a way, it is the opposite of the other stage. In the previous one, we got fully into the ego and strengthened it. Instead, at this stage, we detach ourselves from our minds.

Achieving this stage of growth is more difficult to explain because it is more subjective; it is a process that occurs entirely internally in the person. The previous stage is easy to recognize because there are clear actions that let you know if you are fulfilling it. Instead, at this stage, the actions are "internal."

The way we accomplish this stage of letting go is simply one step. Which is to remind ourselves that we are not our mind, that is, we are not our ego. The objective of this stage is to detach ourselves from it.

Achieving this is very simple; we only need a few minutes (or even seconds) of internal reflection to remind ourselves that we are not our minds. We have to remember that it is only a tool that we use to our advantage.

There are many ways to achieve this, and each one has his internal process by which he lets go and reminds himself that a mind is just a tool.

However, I share two very practical actions that will help

you let go:

Thank you: when someone gives you something you say thank you. After an outing to meet women, you are grateful for all that you accomplished, and you are also grateful for rejections and difficult situations. When you have a girlfriend, you thank her every day for having her. When you get a breakthrough in your skills with women, you appreciate it.

Share your knowledge, experiences, and skills: when a friend asks for advice about women, you give it to them. When you are at a party with friends, you are looking to approach women to bring them to the group and introduce them. When you are with a friend and he is doing poorly in an interaction with a woman, you seek help, say, or do something that increases his social value. When a friend with less ability asks you for help to conquer a girl, you help him.

I put examples relating to seduction. However, you can thank and share in any area of your life.

These two actions: thank and share; they automatically train you to let go because to do them, you have to be detached from your ego. It is impossible to thank and share when you are attached to your ego.

When you are fully identified with your mind, it is as if you are trapped within it. When you are trapped inside your mind, it is impossible to say "thank you" because you only consider what you do not have and what you need. On the other hand, you cannot share either because of that state, and you only seek to obtain things for yourself.

Instead, thanking and sharing automatically lead you to disidentify with your mind and leave the ego. They are actions that, to perform them, require being in a state in which you do not identify with your mind but experience it only as a tool.

The dark side of seduction: when we forget to let go

Now that I have explained the two phases of growth, I can explain much better what I mean by "falling on the dark side of seduction."

To grow healthy, you need to go through these two stages constantly. First comes a stage of ego strengthening, and then it must be accompanied by another in which we let go. When we start to go to an extreme and focus on just one stage of growth, we start having trouble making progress.

If we start to strengthen the ego without letting go, then we will have problems. On the other hand, if we start letting go all the time without strengthening our ego, we will also have problems. Each end will cause different problems when we seek to progress.

To clarify, neither of the two stages is bad. Each one is just as important and necessary. If you have read about personal growth, it may shock you a little when I say that it is important to strengthen the ego. As I said before, it is common for the ego to be interpreted as something evil since there is a lot of information that refers to it as something evil that must be destroyed and eliminated.

The ego (mind) is not bad, and it is necessary to evolve. Nor is it bad to seek to strengthen our ego. The bad thing is when we forget the other part of growth, which is letting go. To grow healthy and progress towards our goals, the two stages of growth are necessary.

At each stage, one enters a different state of mind that is necessary for growth. When we strengthen the ego, we focus on ourselves, and we focus on acquiring resources and becoming more efficient. When we let go, we focus on others, we focus more on sharing the resources we have accumulated, and we become more powerful.

Now falling on the dark side of seduction means forgetting the stage of letting go and getting stuck in the stage of permanently strengthening the ego.

In the seduction case, when we fall on the dark side, we desperately seek to progress to find the confidence and happiness that we dream of obtaining from the beginning. As we make a little progress with women, we realize that we are not obtaining the confidence and happiness that we seek, so we began to look harder to grow faster.

Little by little, we are progressing; each time we start to get better results, we become more efficient. We started to achieve things that we thought were impossible, such as kissing unknown women, generating a lot of attraction in them in a few minutes, and having sex with them the same day we met them.

But as we progress and achieve more, we realize that we have not yet achieved the confidence and happiness that we seek. This becomes an endless cycle of suffering because we always believe that confidence and happiness will be found when we reach a certain level of ability and obtain certain results.

We become obsessed with obtaining better results. We are always looking for better women and doing more impressive things on a social level because we believe that when we advance enough, we will finally get the confidence and happiness we are looking for.

Many have fallen victim to this way of acting. They start to get excellent results with women and achieve things that very few men achieve with girls, but instead of becoming more confident and happier, they become more fearful and unhappy.

It is something very hard to experience; when one falls into this pattern of suffering, it is difficult to overcome it. It is also very difficult to see how close friends destroy your life by falling into this cycle.

The way out of the dark

The way to overcome this endless cycle of suffering is to let go. The problem is that it is difficult to do it when we have been stuck for a long time, strengthening our ego. These two stages of growth are like a synchronous car. It is necessary to stay at a certain speed, but there comes a time when it is necessary to change gear to enter the next stage. If we forget to put the change, then the car begins to suffer.

The problem with being stuck for a long time in the ego-strengthening stage is that as time passes, it becomes more difficult to change in and move on to the stage of letting go. The more months and years we spend staking strengthening the ego indefinitely, the more difficult it is to let go again.

This occurs because as time passes, our suffering begins to grow. Our unhappiness and anxiety begin to increase when we get stuck, strengthening the ego indefinitely. So the more unhappy and fearful we become, the more difficult it makes us let go.

When we are unhappy and afraid, the last thing we want to do is thank and share with others or any other action that helped us let go. Paradoxically, what we least want to do when we are stuck in our minds will help us focus and continue growing healthily.

The solution to this endless cycle of pain is to let go, either by thanking, sharing, or taking time to reflect. We need to distance ourselves from our minds and remember that we are not our knowledge, experiences, skills, or results. All these things are simply tools, but they are not us.

We have to see our mind as if it were a sword. When we have a sword, we can perfect it, reform it, sharpen it, and polish it to make it better. We can do the same with our minds, and we can perfect it. The problem is that unlike the sword, our mind is something very close to us, and in the process of improving it, we forget that it is just a tool.

Being very close to us, then it is very easy to identify with it as we perfect it. The more we perfect it, the greater our tendency to identify with it. However, we can always remember that it is only a tool; it is like a sword that we use to obtain certain things.

Getting the experiences and results you are looking for with women will strengthen your ego and get the amount of sex you are looking for. However, it will not give you the confidence and happiness you are looking for. This is something that you will only find as you increase your ability to let go.

Letting go is an internal skill that must be practiced constantly, especially after very intense stages of ego strengthening. Otherwise, you are going to start falling on the dark side.

If you are someone who already has experience in this game and have obtained great results with women but still feel unhappy and insecure, you need to learn to let go. You have to start thinking and sharing more. I know it's the last thing you're going to want to do if you've been trapped in that cycle of suffering for a while, but it's the only way out.

If you are just beginning, then always remember that you have to complete the stage of letting go so that you can grow and evolve healthily. Above all, remember it in intense stages of growth, for example, when you go out almost every day for months in a row to improve your skills with women. In those intense stages of growth is when it is easier to start forgetting that your mind is just a tool.

It is very hard to see how a great initial dream begins to turn into a nightmare as one progresses. I want your dream of progress to stay the same and keep motivating you day by day in a healthy way. To achieve this, you must always remember the stage of letting go.

CHAPTER 12

START YOUR MENTAL GAME

Imagine that you go to dinner with your partner; you go to a restaurant, observe the environment, they serve you the food, you smell and taste the food, you feel how your partner looks at you, and emotion is born in you... This whole situation triggers a series of stored data in our minds, which gives rise to different mental processes.

How are mental processes defined?

Mental processes are ways in which our mind stores, processes or translates the data provided by our senses to be used at present or in the future. The mind is defined as a set of mental processes.

What characteristics do mental processes have?

Three different characteristics of mental processes can be distinguished:

Intentionality. It refers to the direction towards an object. For example, in love, there is an intention towards something or someone who is loved. Intentionality is precisely what differentiates a physical phenomenon from a psychological one. Intentionality presupposes an attitude: I think, I hope that...

Consciousness. It involves realizing or knowing our mental processes. One can also speak of direct consciousness, referring to an object and reflex consciousness, which refers to a certain mental process.

The representational character. It is a fundamental characteristic of mental processes; if we think of a pool, we do not have a pool in mind, it is simply a representation of that object.

Types of mental processes

Among the mental processes, we can highlight the following:

Intelligence. It involves an ability to recognize what we feel, to find our motivation. Intelligence is not based only on knowledge and skills; it is based on knowing how to manage our own emotions and understand others (emotional intelligence).

The learning. It is a process by which behaviors, knowledge, beliefs, and values are acquired. It can be learned in many ways, through observation, study, or experience, among others.

The feeling. It supposes the result of an emotion.

The emotion. Emotions guide our behavior and influence our thoughts. An emotion can bring us closer to a person, an environment, or an object or, on the contrary, move us away. Emotions, therefore, have psychological, physiological, and behavioral effects.

Perception. It allows us to see and realize what is happening in a given situation. It helps us interpret and give meaning to a situation.

Awareness. It is not a type of mental process, but a set of mental processes that involve various aspects such as physiological or reason. Based on consciousness, a person can act in one way and another, in a different way. The ways of acting, therefore, can be determined by our genetics and by what we learn through our lives.

Attention. It assumes that our mind is focused on a specific stimulus.

As you can see, the mental processes are multiple and sometimes quite complex, so it is a challenge to know them and to know how they work in each person.

Five tips to win at mind games

Never underestimate the playfulness of spirit. Here are a few tips that you can use to win the upper hand.

Do not underestimate the impact of small mental activity. While 'Towergate' may be the direction of Roger Federer to threaten Novak Djokovic with a little psychological warfare right before they were about to face off, not every game of mental thinking should have an evil genius. Mind hacking can help you in business, not through manipulation, but through understanding how your mind functions. This can help you to prevent a difficult situation and get to know your reactions.

Mind Hack 1

Your opponent is a mirror. It helps to reflect your body language when you talk to someone older to you. This helps build a sense of familiarity and comfort as our brains like to assume that they are like us when someone acts like us. But don't go over the top and immediately mimic their shifts in body language. This small hack is particularly good for raising or leaving. They see you like them by looking at their body language.

Mind Hack 2

Only take your time. Take your time. It works better than any serum of reality. Do not prompt additional questions when you ask someone a question about a touchy subject and they respond with an unclear response. Just wait a few moments, and in those awkward silence between you both, more information is usually bubbling than was desired.

Mind Hack 3

President, for you, this one. Limit your options. When you want to convince someone to do something, it is nice to limit their choices and make them know they are doing what they want. They do what they want. When choices are made, people typically stick to the options given, as it is difficult and hostile to offer others.

Mind Hack 4

Sit high. Workers be careful if your boss is trying this psychological trick. You will almost always find that the guy in your highest position sits on a better chair above yours when he joins your boss for a meeting, an interview, or a conference. The guest should be bullied. Counter it with the same height as the employer by adjusting the chair. Ha!

Mind Hack 5

Ask, and you shall receive. When asking your boss or colleague for a favor, start big, and then go small. Starting with a big favor, which you know they are likely to say no to, means that they will feel bad and agree to the smaller one. And if they say yes to you at first, well, that's a win-win situation.

Keep your mind active: tips to preserve memory

Challenge your senses in every possible way; the mental activity is necessary not only to avoid boredom but also to stimulate abilities and prevent cognitive decline.

Here are some tips to keep your mind active and, while you're at it, feel more attentive to what's going on around you, focused and sharp.

Use your brain. It seems like a no-brainer, but if you don't use it, you lose it. Exercising your brain helps maintain your mental acuity. People who often practice mind-challenging activities are the fittest. There are many to choose from, and they don't have to be complex: reading books, listening to the radio, playing games, visiting museums, learning another language...

Change your way of acting, challenge your senses. Do you remember when you were a child and tried to speak backward? Researchers from Duke University (USA) created exercises called "neurobics" to challenge the mind and force it to find new ways of thinking. Your five senses are the key to learning, so you can use them to exercise your mind. If you are right-handed, try to use your left hand. Go to work by a different path than the one you usually use.

Close your eyes, and try to recognize foods for their taste. These are small challenges for your senses that help keep your brain in shape.

Physical exercise to stay alert. Exercise, especially the ones that raise the heart rate, such as walking or swimming, also provides mental benefits. Experts aren't sure why, but the truth is that physical activity increases blood flow in the brain and improves the links between brain cells. Staying active can help memory, imagination, and even the ability to plan tasks.

A healthy diet to improve your intellectual capacity. Do your brain a favor and choose healthy heart and waist foods. Obesity in middle age multiplies the odds of dementia later by two. High cholesterol and hypertension also increase that risk, believe it or not, because they negatively affect neurons. Try cooking your food in the oven or on the grill instead of frying them. Cook with "good" fats, such as olive oil, and avoid butter and fats from meat. Eat fruits and vegetables of all colors. Include fish in your diet.

Watch what you drink. Drinking alcohol affects judgment, speech, movement, and memory. But did you know that it also has long-term effects? If you drink too much for a long time, the size of your brain's frontal lobes may be reduced. And the damage can last forever.

Video games to train your brain. Take the "joystick," and let's play! Several studies claim that playing video games stimulates the brain's areas that control movement, memory, planning, and fine motor skills. Some experts do not share this opinion. The results are not conclusive, but why not try the fun?

Music helps your mind. Thank your mother for insisting on signing up for piano or guitar lessons. Playing an instrument as a child is worth it because it stimulates mental functions such as memory and the ability to plan. It also favors greater coordination between the hands. Plus, it's fun, and it's never too late to start.

Make Friends. Be a friendly person, relate to your environment. Talking to others sharpens your brain, whether at work, at home, or on the street. Studies show that social activity improves your mind. Think about whether you want to volunteer, sign up for a course or workshop, or call a friend!

Stay calm. Too much stress can damage your gray matter, which contains the cells that store and process information. You can relax in many ways: Take deep breaths, find something that makes you laugh, listen to music, try yoga or meditation, or find someone to talk to.

Sleep to take care of your brain. You have to get enough sleep before and after learning something new because it helps the brain learn. If you start tired, it is difficult to concentrate. Sleeping after learning something allows the brain to fix that knowledge so you can get it back later. A good night's rest is the best thing you can do for your memory and also for your mood. An adult needs 7 to 8 hours of sleep each night.

Tricks for memory. Everyone is distracted from time to

time. As you get older, it becomes more difficult to remember things, and it is not as easy as before. It is a normal situation that happens to many older people. To avoid this forgetfulness affecting your daily life, you can: Write down what you don't want to be forgotten. Use the calendar and reminder function on your phone, even for simple things ("Call Mom"). Concentrate on a single task, avoiding several at once. Learning new things step by step, even if it is slower, will be easier for you.

The game of names. Do you have difficulty remembering names? Repeat the name of the person you are talking to several times throughout the conversation, at least in your head, if you don't want to do it out loud. You can also make up a picture or a simple rhyme that you can relate to their name.

CHAPTER 13

HOW TO DISTINGUISH BETWEEN PERSUASION AND MANIPULATION

Not all appear to be deceptive in non-rational conditions.

Calling a person dishonest is a critique of the character of the individual. The complaint that you were mistreated is simply a complaint. Manipulation is at best unreliable and at worst unethical. What is that, however? What makes manipulation wrong? Human beings always and in all sorts of ways influence each other. But what differentiates and makes manipulation immoral from other influences?

Attempts to exploit us are continuous. Here are some examples. Some situations involve encouraging someone to doubt their judgment and trust the manipulator's advice. Guilt trips make someone feel excessively guilty for not doing what the manipulator wants them to do. Spell offensives and peer pressure induce someone to worry so much about the manipulator's approval that they will do what the manipulator wants.

Advertising manipulates when it encourages the audience to form false beliefs. When we are told to believe that fried chicken is a healthy food, or defective association, as when Marlboro cigarettes are linked to the robust vigor of the Marlboro Man. Phishing and other scams manipulate their victims through a combination of deception (forged telephone numbers or URLs) and play with emotions like greed, fear, or sympathy.

Then there is a more direct manipulation; perhaps the most famous example is when Yago manipulates Othello to create suspicions about Desdemona's fidelity, play with his insecurities to make him jealous, and load him with a rage that leads Othello to murder his beloved. All of these examples of manipulation share a sense of immortality.

What do they have in common?

Manipulation is not always harmful

Perhaps manipulation is wrong because it hurts the person being manipulated. Certainly, manipulation often hurts. If successful, cigarette manipulative ads contribute to illness and death; use of phishing, malware, and other types of identity robbery; social media can promote hostile or unhealthy relations, and political manipulation can encourage discord and undermine democracy. Manipulation, however, is not always dangerous.

Suppose Amy's abusive partner has been abandoned, but in a moment of weakness, she will be tempted to return to him. Imagine now that Amy's friends use the same techniques as Othello used for Lago. They manipulate Amy so that she (falsely) believes and is outraged that her ex-partner was abusive and unfaithful. If this manipulation prevents Amy from reconciling, it could be better than if her friends hadn't manipulated her. However, to many, it could still seem morally dangerous. Intuitively, her friends would have been morally safer to use non-manipulation to help

Amy avoid recurrence. However, when these benefits rather hurt the exploited individual, something remains morally questionable about manipulation.

So the damage may not be the reason why manipulation is wrong.

Perhaps the manipulation is wrong because it involves inherently immoral techniques of treating other human beings. This thought might be especially attractive to those inspired by Immanuel Kant's idea that morality requires that we treat each other as rational beings rather than mere objects. Perhaps the only adequate way to influence other rational beings' behavior is through rational persuasion, and therefore any form of influence other than rational persuasion is morally improper. But despite its appeal, this answer also falls short, as it would condemn many morally benign forms of influence.

For example, much of Lago's manipulation involves appealing to Othello's emotions. But emotional appeals are not always manipulative. Moral persuasion often appeals to empathy or conveys how it would feel to have others do what you are doing to them. Similarly, making someone fear something really dangerous, feeling guilty about something immoral, or feeling a reasonable level of confidence in one's real abilities does not appear to be manipulation. Even invitations to doubt your judgment may not be manipulative in situations where, perhaps due to intoxication or strong emotions, there are good reasons to do so.

Not all forms of non-rational influence appear to be manipulative.

It seems, then, that whether an influence is manipulative depends on how it is used. Iago's actions are manipulative and wrong because they are meant to make Othello think and feel the wrong things. Iago knows that Othello doesn't have to be jealous, but he still makes Othello jealous. This is the emotional analog of deception that Iago also practices when he fixes things (for example, the fallen handkerchief) to trick Othello into forming beliefs that Iago knows to be false. The central point of manipulation occurs when the manipulator tricks another into distrusting what the manipulator recognizes as good judgment. In contrast, advising an angry friend to avoid making quick judgments before calming down is not manipulative, if you know that your friend's judgment is temporarily inappropriate.

But moral persuasion rather than manipulation is a strong call for empathy for real persons who suffer from unexpected misery. If an abusive partner attempts to make you feel bad about the presumption of unfaithfulness that they already have, they are deceptive, and they try to deceive guilt. However, when a friend makes you feel guilty of having left him in his time of need, it does not seem manipulative.

What manipulates the power and does not do it is the same: the manipulator tries to adopt what the manipulator regards as an inappropriate belief, emotion, or another state of mind. In this way, manipulation resembles lying. What makes a statement a lie and morally wrong is the same: for the speaker to try to get someone to adopt what he considers to be a false belief. In both cases, the intention is to get someone else to make some kind of mistake. The liar tries to make you adopt a false belief. The manipulator could do that, but he could also try to make you feel inappropriate emotion (or inappropriately strong or weak), attaching too much importance to the wrong things (for example, the approval of another person) or doubting something (for example, your judgment or the fidelity of your beloved) of whom there is no good reason to doubt. The difference between manipulation and non-manipulation depends on how a person wants to make anything of what they think, feel, doubt, or care about.

In addition to pure rational conviction, we influence one another in a human condition. It is endemic.

These factors often enhance the decision taking situation of the other person by making them believe, doubt, or feel or be vigilant about the right things; often, they undermine decision-making by making them believe, doubt, or feel that the wrong things are done. However, manipulation requires the deliberate use of these forces to prevent an individual from making the right decision: this is the basic immorality of manipulation.

This manipulative way of thinking tells us how to recognize it. Manipulation is a form of control, and it is tentative to think. As we have shown, without manipulation, the forms of stimuli that can be used for handling can be implemented. It is not what power is used to define coercion, but how the effect is used to make a decision better or worse for the other person. And we should not look at the type of power to understand exploitation. However, the purpose of the individual using it is the root and inherent immorality of coercion, as it is meant to undermine someone else's decision-making situation.

A matter of ethics

We all need to convince others to come up with some proposal of ours. From the seller who tries to get his client to choose the brand he promotes, the publicist who seeks to increase the consumption of a product, the politician who wants to win the votes of citizens, to the director who tries to convince his staff of the vision he has created for the company coming true.

All this indicates that persuasion is a subject of great use and utility. This led to social psychology and communication research, and a range of techniques have been developed for making convincing messages more effective. But it has been left aside on several occasions, be it ethical or not to use this device. This section aims to identify the differences between manipulation and ethical persuasion and invite the reader to avoid the first and make use of the second.

General Persuasion and Ethical Persuasion

The principle of persuasion should first be described. Collins (2009, p. 4) states that persuasion is "a change, intentional and internalized, in attitude, belief or conduct, that is, a communication that gives the beneficiary a certain degree of choice freedom." For example, Cablevisión, with its television advertisements, intends that Internet users cancel the service that Telmex provided and switch to Yoo, for which they offer a series of arguments, including speed and cost. Here it is intended to achieve a change in the belief that the fastest Internet service is that of Telmex so that the user transforms behavior and leaves one provider for another; his motto is "Change now."

Upon analyzing the concept of persuasion explained previously, we discover that it has no ethical consideration. Rather, one would speak of effective or ineffective persuasion, depending on whether they have achieved their purpose. Gadner (2004, p.212) expresses this practical conception of the art of persuading in the following words: "It is up to us to choose the use that we give (to the techniques of persuasion) and to do it selfishly and destructively, or in a way that is generous and makes improvements in life." In this way, the techniques proposed by the communication theorists would be neither good nor bad, since their ethical value would depend on the purpose for which they were used. From this perspective, the end would justify the means.

On the contrary, several authors (Messina 2007, Reardon 1991) insist that persuasion must be applied with ethical parameters. Among them, Baker and Martinson (2001) stand out, who propose that for persuasion to be ethical, five principles must be met:

- **The truthfulness of the message:** Telling the truth without distorting the information.
- **The authenticity of the one who seeks to persuade:** Be genuine and act in harmony with

what one believes.

- **Respect for the recipients:** That they are treated as ends and not as means; avoid using them for personal benefit or the company.
- **Fair use of the persuasive message's appeal:** Avoids just talking about the positives of the proposal. Especially with vulnerable audiences, such as children and people with little education. They must be treated according to their limitations to understand the costs and potential harm they are asked to do. Otherwise, persuasion would be abusive and manipulative.
- **Social responsibility:** It is necessary to consider the effects of persuasive communication on the community and society as a whole. It would be unethical to try to achieve a company's sales goals or profitability at the expense of the common good.

In summary, it can be affirmed that, for persuasion to be ethical, it must respect the recipient's dignity, allowing him to make a voluntary, informed, rational and reflective choice.

If we analyze the great deceptions that some pseudo-entrepreneurs or directors of companies have carried out, we see that they have been efficient in their persuasion attempt, but unethical. For example, the fraud carried out by the private investment fund company Stanford Investment that offered investors the promise of extraordinary profits, higher than the average of the financial instruments available in the Mexican market (very well marked the benefits of its proposal). Still, they failed to say that the Mexican Stock exchange institution was not registered, and if losses were incurred, no institution would protect them. His proposal was deceptive and manipulative. The result was that investors lost their money and couldn't find a way to get it back. As for the company director, he was left as a scoundrel, who has closed the doors to return to do business in Mexico and many countries of the world. When we see so many forms of deceit and manipulations in the business world, it would seem that the human being has a malicious pixie that leads him to want to abuse others, to achieve wealth or power quickly. But the wise part of the human being seeks to counteract that pixie through laws and regulatory institutions.

There are accounts of several brokers in Mexico who want to encourage potential clients to invest in their business instead of Stanford Investment. They accept their plan for sound reasons, backed by comparative performance figures on the market for their funds. When talking to the customer, they show enthusiasm about their products and make explicit the benefits they will obtain, avoiding deception and, above all, respecting the person's freedom. The consequence of this ethical persuasion will be that the client will have trust and loyalty with the institution and with the executive, which will allow them to continue doing business with them, instead of leaving with the competition. In the long run, ethical persuasion pays off.

How to Protect Yourself from Unethical Persuasion

While there is an ethical responsibility in the persuader, the recipient also has to do his part: protect himself from abusive and deceptive attempts at persuasion. To achieve this, Pratkanis and Aronson (2001) suggest that we take the following measures:

Know the ways of persuasion and recognize that one can be a victim of propaganda. For example, we can develop the habit of analyzing ads that offer products that seem magical (such as those that promise to erase wrinkles in 60 seconds) and wonder if they will do everything that the advert promises.

Monitor our emotions. If you feel that your emotions have been played with, get out of that situation and analyze what is happening to you. For example, if you find that you have been scared or guilty about buying a service, consider whether you need it.

Explore the motivations and credibility of the source of the communication. Ask yourself if the communicator is an expert and trustworthy. For example, it is obvious that a seller is interested in closing the sale to earn the commission, so we may doubt that he wants to help us choose the product that best meets our needs, even if the competition sells it.

Think rationally about the proposal they make to you. Take on the devil's advocate's role and reflect on the arguments against what you are being asked to do, the seller will tell you about all its benefits, and it is up to you to identify all its defects.

Review the full range of alternatives before making a decision. Do market research before buying a good or service. For example, if you have decided to buy a laptop, visit several stores and check several brands to compare the price and the functions they offer.

Do not base your evaluation on what the persuader says, but on what he does. For example, if Televisa stresses in its propaganda that the mass media have a social commitment, and we observe that the company supports campaigns like the Telethon, we can believe their words.

If the proposal is too beautiful to be true, it may be misleading. If Stanford Investment investors had followed this recommendation, they might not have lost their money.

Human beings like others to do what they ask of them, be they an entrepreneur, a publicist, a manager, or a politician. To achieve this, you can apply the principles and fundamentals of effective persuasion, regardless of deception or manipulation. The unethical persuader may accomplish his or her purpose. Still, as soon as the recipients become aware of the abuse, the trust will be broken, and it will be almost impossible to restore it. In the business world, trust is essential. If a manager or company director speaks the truth, is authentic, respects his clients' dignity, and his employees, they will trust him, and they will be able to establish lasting relationships. Ethical persuasion has its costs, but it is well worth paying?

CHAPTER 14

CONCLUSION

We are used to thinking that we own our body and mind; after all, who else would it belong to, if not us? However, our mind is somewhat confusing and complex since it keeps many secrets in it that until today have not been fully discovered. And what's even more interesting is that it can manipulate us when we least expect it. For example, if we are hesitant about starting a new job in something completely unfamiliar to us, the good news is that this means we are more likely to succeed in doing so. So in this final chapter of this book, we have compiled ten quite curious mind games that our mind plays on us without us knowing.

Halo effect

It is a popular and well-known influence by marketers and advertisers; behind this is the belief that a person can easily determine a product or service based on an individual. Therefore we have many supermodels and actresses who are the "face" of great make-up lines or clothing companies. We like to assume that renowned people have the slogan "I cannot do something wrong," and unintentionally pass it to the product they want to sell. In general, we are less stringent with famous or recognized characters than we will ever punish ordinary people when it comes to some form of crime or accident.

Spectator effect

This psychological effect is a bit sad: While in a crowd of people, a person is less likely to help someone who needs it because we unconsciously believe that someone else will. A few years ago, several experiments were carried out on this effect and revealed that when one person in the crowd decides to help in an emergency, others immediately followed his behavior. But the most difficult and most important thing was to find the "hero" to start the movement.

Spotlight effect or epicenter effect

Have you ever thought too much about the impression you make on others? Did you think you were too clumsy or did you wear the best outfit for the party? This is known as the Spotlight effect, we literally think all the time that we are the center of attention and that any missteps we take are immediately going to be noticed by other people. This psychological effect tricks our minds into believing that people fixate on ourselves as much as we do, and that everything we do will be judged and examined by other people when, in reality, this mental exaggeration is far from true.

Disinhibition effect on networks

The media have contributed greatly to the development of this effect behind online "trolls" and cyberbullying. On the Internet, where we can use an alias, we tend to be more severe, critical, and harsh than we normally are in real life. It is much easier than doing it face to face, and not everyone can resist the temptation to show their anger instead of being calm and polite.

The "cheerleader" effect

Aren't cheerleaders beautiful? We are not all so exceptionally beautiful, and it is the "animating effect" or "attractive effect" that is a huge help in the field of public relations. So much so that it was given that name. The essence of the effect is this: a person appears to be more beautiful when surrounded by a group of attractive friends; It is also known as the "group attraction effect." This happens because your brain calculates the "average attractiveness level" in the group you are in.

The Dunning-Kruger effect or syndrome

This is a very peculiar thing. Have you ever seen someone who is inexperienced in a specific field and who has rarely, without any knowledge, been very successful in doing this? Conversely, a professional in your field, struggling for years to succeed without being able to make further progress? It's Dunning-Kruger, which explains how beginners have a breakthrough in any area because, unlike professionals who know all things already, they're less familiar with limitations and rules.

Déjà vu

Most of us know this French term that means "something already seen." Déjà vu is the feeling that you have already experienced a situation happening to you in real-time. Before psychology gave it this name, the déjà vu effect made people believe they had a first psychic experience as if they were witnessing a warning or a prophecy. Psychology still does not have a clear answer to the question that we all ask ourselves: What triggers these feelings? To this day, the déjà vu effect remains an unsolved phenomenon.

Google effect

For so long, Google has made a major contribution to the trend of information being lost easily, especially when we are confident that everything is quickly accessible on the Internet. This is why this effect is known as the Influence of Google.

Pareidolia

Taking advantage of the use of Latin words, pareidolia is an effect that makes us see things that are familiar to us in unknown or unusual places.

The phenomenon of the broken ladder

This phenomenon deceives our physical reaction. That's when we expect something to happen, but this isn't going to happen. It is most evident in scenarios such as when we wait for the last step when we go down the stairs, and it is not there, or when we step on a broken escalator, and it does not move. Our body begins to feel nauseous or like we are tripping over our own feet, or that we are losing our balance; this is exactly what the "phenomenon of broken escalators" is.

Have you ever experienced any of these phenomena? Try to remember when you first fell into a trap that your mind played on you.

www.ingramcontent.com/pod-product-compliance
Lightning Source LLC
Chambersburg PA
CBHW060317030426
42336CB00011B/1094